MATH

by Ellen Carley Frechette

LiteracyLink is a joint project of the PBS, Kentucky Educational Television, the National Center on Adult Literacy, and the Kentucky Department of Education. This project is funded in whole, or in part, by the Star Schools Program of the USDE under contract #R203D60001.

Acknowledgments

LiteracyLink® Advisory Board

Dr. Drew Albritton, American Association for
    Adult and Continuing Education
Peggy Barber, American Library Association
Anthony Buttino, WNED-TV
Dr. Anthony Carnevale, Educational Testing Service
Dr. Patricia Edwards, Michigan State University
Maggi Gaines, Baltimore Reads, Inc.
Dr. Milton Goldberg, National Alliance for Business
Columbus Hartwell, Exodus
Jan Hawkins, Center for Children and Technology,
    Education Development Corporation, Inc.
Neal Johnson, Educational Testing Service
Dr. Cynthia Johnston, Central Piedmont
    Community College
Thomas Kinney, American Association of Adult
    and Continuing Education
Dr. Jacqueline E. Korengel, Kentucky Department
    for Adult Ed and Literacy
Michael O'Brian, Certain Teed Corporation
Rafael Ramirez, U.S. Deptartment of Education
Dr. Emma Rhodes, Formerly of Arkansas Department
    of Education
Dr. Ahmed Sabie, Kentucky Department of Adult
    Education and Literacy
Tony Sarmiento, Worker Centered Learning,
    Working for America Institute *
Dr. Steve Steurer, Correctional Education Association
Dr. Alice Tracy, Correctional Education Association
Dr. Fran Tracy-Mumford, Delaware Department of
    Adult/Community Education
Dr. Terilyn Turner, Community Education, St. Paul
    Public Schools
Dr. Renee Westcott, Central Piedmont Community
    College

Ex Officio Advisory Members

Joan Aucher, GED Testing Service
Cheryl Garnette, U.S. Department of Education
Dr. Andrew Hartman, National Institute for Literacy
Dr. Mary Lovell, U.S. Department of Education
Ronald Pugsley, U.S. Department of Education
Dr. Linda Roberts, U.S. Department of Education
Joe Wilkes, U.S. Department of Education

LiteracyLink Partners

LiteracyLink is a joint project of the Public Broadcasting
Service, Kentucky Educational Television, the National
Center on Adult Literacy, and the Kentucky Department
of Education. This project is funded in whole, or in part,
by the Star Schools Program of the USDE under contract
#R203D60001.

Special thanks to the Kentucky Department for
Adult Education and Literacy, Workforce Development
Cabinet for its help on this project and for its vision and
commitment to excellence in helping provide superior
adult education products and services.

Workbook Production

Developer:
Learning Unlimited, Oak Park, Illinois

Design:
PiperStudios Inc., Chicago, Illinois

Cover Design and Layout:
By Design, Lexington, Kentucky

Project Consultant:
Milli Fazey, KET, Lexington, Kentucky

Production Manager:
Margaret Norman, KET, Lexington, Kentucky

• •

Copyright © 1999, Public Broadcasting Service
All rights reserved.

PBS *LiteracyLink, LitTeacher, LitLearner, LitHelper* and *PeerLit* are registered marks of the Public Broadcasting Service.

No part of this book may be reproduced or transmitted in any form or by any means, electronic or mechanical, including
photocopying, recording, or by any information storage and retrieval without permission in writing from the publisher.

Printed in the United States of America.

ISBN 1-881020-37-1

Table of Contents

To the Teacher

The purpose of the *Workplace Essential Skills* series is to enable adult learners to become better informed and more highly skilled for the changing world of work. The materials are aimed at adults who are at the pre-GED (6th- to 8th-grade) reading level.

Twenty-four *Workplace Essential Skills* **television programs** model the application of basic skills within the context of pre-employment and workplace settings. The four accompanying **workbooks** present instruction, practice, and application of the critical skills that are represented in the programs:

- *Employment*
- *Communication & Writing*
- *Reading*
- *Mathematics*

The series includes a utilization program for instructors and an overview program for learners.

The series also includes a **teacher's guide** for instructors and an **assessment instrument** to help learners and instructors determine the most effective course of study in the *Workplace Essential Skills* series.

Each lesson in the *Math* workbook corresponds to one of the five math television programs in the *Workplace Essential Skills* series. The topics in the *Math* workbook and the video programs are based on common labor market and workplace tasks.

Basic skills, problem solving, and decision making are integrated into every lesson. Additionally, interdisciplinary connections are inserted throughout the books for practice in real-world reading, writing, communication, math, and technology skills.

Taken together, the features and components of the *Workplace Essential Skills* instructional program provide a comprehensive grounding in the knowledge and skills learners need to succeed in the world of work. By also utilizing the *LiteracyLink* on-line component (see page vii), learners will begin to develop some of the computer literacy and Internet know-how needed to advance in the workplace of today and tomorrow.

Many of the skills covered in *Workplace Essential Skills* also provide a foundation for GED-level work in the areas of reading, math, and writing. Because high school completion is an important prerequisite for advancement in the work world, learners should be encouraged to go on to GED-level study when they are ready to do so. The *LiteracyLink* GED videos, print, and on-line materials (available in the year 2000) will provide an ideal context for learners to prepare for the GED tests and fulfill the requirement of high school equivalency.

To the Learner

Welcome to *Workplace Essential Skills: Math.* This workbook has been designed to help you learn more about the ideas and skills presented in Programs 20-24 of the *Workplace Essential Skills* series. Take time to read about some of the features in this book.

1. The **Skills Preview** on pages 1-11 will help you discover which video programs and workbook lessons are most important for you. You can use the **Skills Preview Evaluation Chart** on page 12 to make your own personal study plan.

2. Each workbook lesson goes with a program in the television series. The lessons in this workbook cover Programs 20-24. Use the program number and title to find the corresponding tape and workbook lesson. After the opening page and **Objectives,** each lesson is divided into two parts:

    Before You Watch starts you thinking about the topics in the video program.

    - **Sneak Preview:** Exercise to preview some of the key concepts from the program.
    - **Answers for Sneak Preview:** Answers to the preview exercise.
    - **Feedback:** Information to help you personalize your work.
    - **Vocabulary:** Key terms from the lesson and their definitions.

    After You Watch allows you to apply skills that you saw in the program.

    - **Key Points from the Video Program:** List that summarizes the program.
    - **Situations:** Real-world problem solving from the health care, manufacturing, service, retail, and construction industries.
    - **Information:** In-depth information about important workplace concepts.
    - **WorkTips:** Hints for success in the world of work.
    - **WorkSkills:** Exercise that enables you to apply what you have learned.
    - **Connections:** Extension of workplace skills through practice in other content areas. (*Write It, Tech Tip, Read It, Math Matters,* and *Communicate*)
    - **Review:** Section that lets you put all of your new workplace knowledge together.

3. The **Skills Review** allows you to evaluate what you have learned.

4. The **Answer Key** starts on page 125. There you can find answers to the exercises in each lesson, often with explanations.

5. The **Glossary,** which starts on page 141, includes key terms and definitions.

6. You can use the alphabetized **Index,** which starts on page 143, to look up information about math-related terms.

7. A **Reference Handbook,** found on pages 145-152, is a helpful resource for you to access at any time. References to the handbook are listed throughout the book.

The LiteracyLink® System

Welcome to the *LiteracyLink* system. This workbook is one part of an educational system for adult learners and adult educators.

LiteracyLink consists of these learning tools:

Television programs
broadcast on public television and in adult learning centers

Computer-based materials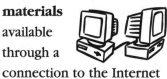
available through a connection to the Internet

Workbooks
print-based instruction and practice

If you are working with *LiteracyLink* materials, you have a clear educational advantage. As you develop your knowledge and skills, you are also working with video and computer technology. This is the technology required to succeed in today's workplace, training programs, and colleges.

Content of the *LiteracyLink* System

The *LiteracyLink* system allows you to choose what you need to meet your goals. It consists of instruction and practice in the areas of:

Workplace Essential Skills
- Employment
  Pre-Employment and On-the-Job Skills
- Communication & Writing
  Listening, Speaking, and Writing Skills
- Reading
  Charts, Forms, Documents, and Manuals
- Mathematics
  Whole Numbers, Decimals, Fractions, and Percents

GED Preparation Series
- Language Arts Reading
  Fiction, Nonfiction, Poetry, Drama and Informational
- Language Arts Writing
  Essay Writing, Sentence Structure, Grammar, and Mechanics
- Social Studies
  U.S. History, World History, Geography, Civics and Government, and Economics
- Science
  Life Sciences, Earth and Space Sciences, Chemistry, and Physics
- Mathematics
  Arithmetic, Data Analysis, Algebra, and Geometry

Instructional Units

Units of study are used to organize *LiteracyLink's* instruction. For example, the first unit in this book is Number Sense. To study this topic, you can use a video, workbook lesson, and computer. You will be able to easily find what you need since each workbook unit has the same title as a video and related Internet activities.

Getting Started With the System

It is possible to use each *LiteracyLink* component separately. However, you will make the best use of *LiteracyLink* if you use all of the parts. You can make this work in a way that is best for you through the *LiteracyLink* Internet site.

On the Internet site, you will take a Welcome Tour and establish your Home Space. The Home Space is your starting point for working through the online portion of *LiteracyLink*. It is also a place where you can save all of your online work.

An important part of the online system is LitHelper℠. This helps you to identify your strengths and weaknesses. LitHelper℠ helps you to develop an individualized study plan. The online LitLearner® materials, together with the videos and workbooks, provide hundreds of learning opportunities. Go to http://www.pbs.org/literacy to access the online material.

For Teachers

Parts of *LiteracyLink* have been developed for adult educators and service providers. LitTeacher® is an online professional development system. It provides a number of resources including PeerLit℠ a database of evaluated websites. At http://www.pbs.org/literacy you can also access *LitTeacher*.

Who's Responsible for *LiteracyLink*?

LiteracyLink was sparked by a five-year grant by the U.S. Department of Education. The following partners have contributed to the development of the *LiteracyLink* system:
- PBS Adult Learning Service
- Kentucky Educational Television (KET)
- The National Center on Adult Literacy (NCAL) of the University of Pennsylvania
- The Kentucky Department of Education

The *LiteracyLink* partners wish you the very best in achieving your educational goals.

Skills Preview

The following questions are based on the skills you will learn in video programs 20 through 24 and this book. Answer these questions as best you can. Then check your answers and fill in the evaluation chart on page 12. This will give you a good idea of the skills you need to work on most.

Questions 1–3 are based on this employee wage scale.

# of shifts	1	2	3	4	5
# of hours	8	16	_____	32	40
total pay	$46.40	$ _____	$139.20	$185.60	$232.00

1. Based on this wage scale, how much would an employee earn by working 16 hours?

    (1) $24.20
    (2) $34.10
    (3) $90.20
    (4) $92.80

2. How many hours are there in 3 shifts?

    (1) 24
    (2) 26
    (3) 28
    (4) 30

3. In order to earn $371.20, how many shifts would an employee work?

    (1) 6
    (2) 7
    (3) 8
    (4) 9

Questions 4–10 are based on this store transfer invoice.

SOUTHBURY FARMS STORE

Store Transfer Invoice

Date Shipped: _____

Product	Quantity	Units	Unit Cost	Total Cost
Valencia oranges	12	cases	$ 32.50	$ _____
medium eggs	10	dozen	$ _____	$ 11.90
large eggs	25	dozen	$ 1.20	$ 30.00
seedless grapes	13	pounds	$ 1.98	$ _____
2% milk	20	quarts	$ .75	$ 15.00
salad dressing	_____	bottles	$ .79	$ 15.80
iceberg lettuce	32	heads	$ .89	$ 28.48

---

4. What is the total cost of the 12 cases of Valencia oranges?

   (1) $2.70
   (2) $27.00
   (3) $270.00
   (4) $390.00

5. What is the unit cost of one dozen medium eggs?

   (1) $11.90
   (2) $1.19
   (3) $1.00
   (4) $.90

6. There are 12 eggs in a dozen. How many eggs, including both medium and large, were transferred?

   (1) 420
   (2) 300
   (3) 230
   (4) 35

7. *Estimate* the total cost of the seedless grapes.

   (1) $22.00
   (2) $24.00
   (3) $26.00
   (4) $31.00

8. There are four quarts in one gallon. How many gallons of milk were transferred?

   (1) 5
   (2) 25
   (3) 40
   (4) 80

9. How many bottles of salad dressing were transferred?

   (1) 2
   (2) 14
   (3) 20
   (4) 24

10. Twenty-five percent of the heads of iceberg lettuce that were transferred arrived spoiled. How many heads arrived spoiled?

   (1) 800
   (2) 8
   (3) 7
   (4) 5

Questions 11–13 refer to the following pattern. It gives the proper measurements for a medium-sized sweater.

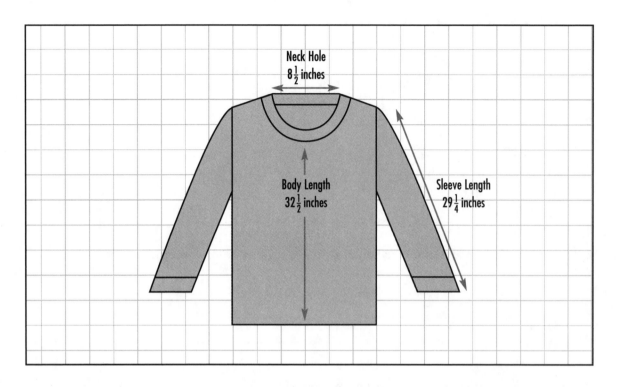

11. The sleeve length of a sweater can be as much as $\frac{3}{8}$ inch longer or shorter than the pattern shows. Is a sweater with a sleeve length of 30 inches acceptable?

    (1) yes
    (2) no

12. A worker knit a sweater that had a neck hole that measured $7\frac{7}{8}$ inches. How many inches smaller is this than the pattern indicates?

    (1) $\frac{1}{8}$
    (2) $\frac{1}{4}$
    (3) $\frac{3}{8}$
    (4) $\frac{5}{8}$

13. One-half of the length of the sweater pictured will be black. How many inches in length will be black?

    (1) $15\frac{1}{2}$
    (2) $16\frac{1}{4}$
    (3) 17
    (4) $17\frac{3}{4}$

Questions 14–16 refer to the following chart used by machinists.

Decimal Equivalents of Drill Sizes	
Drill Number	**Diameter, in inches**
80	0.0135
78	0.016
76	0.02
74	0.0225
72	0.025
70	0.028
68	0.031
66	0.033
64	0.036

14. As the drill numbers get smaller, the diameters

    (1) get smaller
    (2) stay the same
    (3) get larger

15. What is the difference in inches between the diameter of Drill #78 and Drill #74?

    (1) .0065
    (2) .0209
    (3) .0385
    (4) .0415

16. Would a drill with a diameter of 0.027 be smaller or larger than Drill #70?

    (1) smaller
    (2) larger

Questions 17–20 refer to the following quality control time chart.

Shift	Main Work	Handle	Walk	Pack	Wait
A 6:00–10:00 A.M.	2 hours	.5 hour	.25 hour	1 hour	.25 hour
B 10:00 A.M.–2:00 P.M.	2.5 hours	.2 hour	.5 hour	.3 hour	.5 hour
C 2:00–6:00 P.M.	3 hours	.5 hour	.2 hour	.3 hour	0 hours
D 6:00–10:00 P.M.	3.5 hours	.1 hour	.1 hour	.1 hour	.2 hour

17. Between 6:00 A.M. and 10:00 P.M., how many hours were spent waiting?

    (1) .5
    (2) .6
    (3) .75
    (4) .95

18. How much more time was spent waiting during Shift A than Shift D?

    (1) .5 hour
    (2) .05 hour
    (3) .04 hour
    (4) .025 hour

19. What percent of Shift A was spent doing the main work?

    (1) 20%
    (2) 25%
    (3) 50%
    (4) 60%

20. What fraction of the entire day (6:00 A.M.–10:00 P.M.) was spent on main work?

    (1) $\frac{13}{16}$
    (2) $\frac{11}{16}$
    (3) $\frac{5}{8}$
    (4) $\frac{9}{16}$

Questions 21–23 refer to the following graph, which shows the number of coupons that producers have distributed to consumers.

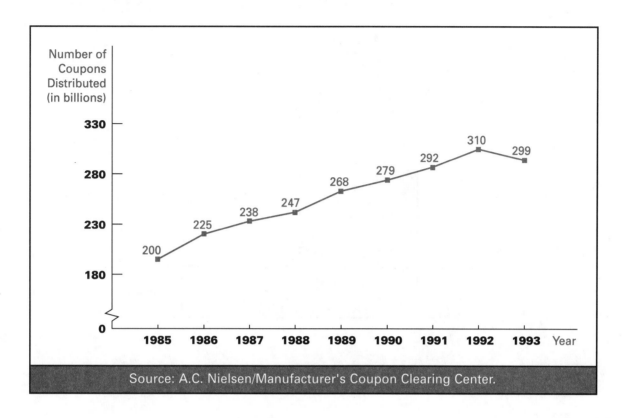

Source: A.C. Nielsen/Manufacturer's Coupon Clearing Center.

21. How many coupons were distributed in 1986?

    (1) 225
    (2) 200 billion
    (3) 225 billion
    (4) 250 billion

22. In what year was the greatest number of coupons distributed?

    (1) 1990
    (2) 1991
    (3) 1992
    (4) 1993

23. Which of the following statements is true based on the graph?

    (1) The number of coupons distributed rose to unexpected heights before declining in 1993.
    (2) The number of coupons distributed rose steadily until 1993.
    (3) The number of coupons distributed exceeded expectations in 1992.
    (4) The number of coupons distributed rose from 1985 to 1992, then fell slightly.

Questions 24–26 refer to the following sketch of an aluminum plate being cut in a metalworking shop.

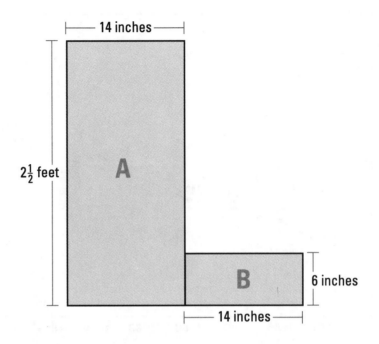

24. How many *feet* is the perimeter of Plate A?

    (1) 5
    (2) $6\frac{1}{3}$
    (3) $7\frac{1}{3}$
    (4) 88

25. What is the area of Plate B?

    (1) 84 sq. in.
    (2) 60 sq. in.
    (3) 40 sq. in.
    (4) 20 sq. in.

26. What will be the length of Plate A and B once they are welded together?

    (1) 28 feet
    (2) 20 feet
    (3) 14 feet
    (4) $2\frac{1}{3}$ feet

Questions 27—29 refer to the following carpenter's drawing of a hole to be cut in a square piece of wood.

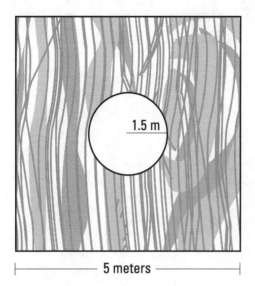

5 meters

27. Which of the following expressions shows the circumference of the hole to be cut?

    (1) $\pi(1.5)$
    (2) $(1.5)^2$
    (3) $\pi(1.5 \times 2)$
    (4) $2(1.5 \times 2)$

28. What is the area of the square?

    (1) 25 sq. meters
    (2) 20 sq. meters
    (3) 15 sq. meters
    (4) 10 sq. meters

29. How many **centimeters** is the perimeter of the square?

    (1) .002
    (2) 20
    (3) 200
    (4) 2000

Questions 30–32 refer to the following graph, which shows when people drink milk.

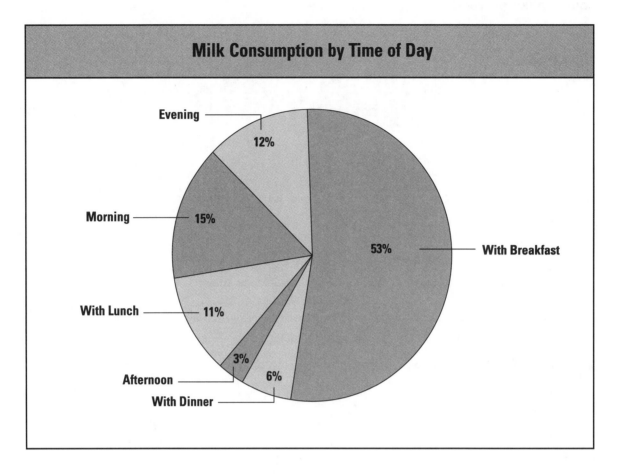

Milk Consumption by Time of Day

Evening 12%

Morning 15%

With Lunch 11%

Afternoon 3%

With Dinner 6%

With Breakfast 53%

30. What fraction of the milk consumed in a day is consumed at breakfast?

    (1) about half

    (2) about one-third

    (3) about one-fourth

    (4) about one-tenth

31. From least to greatest consumption, at what times of day is milk consumed?

    (1) afternoon, with dinner, with lunch, evening, morning, with breakfast

    (2) with dinner, with lunch, afternoon, morning, evening, with breakfast

    (3) with breakfast, morning, evening, with lunch, with dinner, afternoon

    (4) with breakfast, evening, with lunch, afternoon, with dinner, with breakfast

32. Which of the following statements can you conclude by looking at the graph?

    (1) Milk is a popular afternoon drink with children just home from school.

    (2) People are most likely to consume milk with their breakfast.

    (3) Milk is consumed throughout the day because it is the most popular beverage.

    (4) People prefer soft drinks with lunch because they are lower in fat than milk is.

Skills Preview Answer Key

1. (4) $92.80
2. (1) 24
3. (3) 8
4. (4) $390.00
5. (2) $1.19
6. (1) 420
7. (3) $26.00
8. (1) 5
9. (3) 20
10. (2) 8
11. (2) no
12. (4) $\frac{5}{8}$
13. (2) $16\frac{1}{4}$
14. (3) get larger
15. (1) .0065
16. (1) smaller
17. (4) .95

18. (2) .05 hour
19. (3) 50%
20. (2) $\frac{11}{16}$
21. (3) 225 billion
22. (3) 1992
23. (4) The number of coupons distributed rose from 1985 to 1992, then fell slightly.
24. (3) $7\frac{1}{3}$
25. (1) 84 sq. in.
26. (4) $2\frac{1}{3}$ feet
27. (3) $\pi(1.5 \times 2)$
28. (1) 25 sq. meters
29. (4) 2000
30. (1) about half
31. (1) afternoon, with dinner, with lunch, evening, morning, with breakfast
32. (2) People are most likely to consume milk with their breakfast.

Skills Preview Evaluation Chart

Circle the question numbers that you answered correctly. Then fill in the number of questions you got correct for each program lesson. Find the total number correct, and focus your work on the lessons you had trouble with.

Program Lesson	Question Number	Number Correct/Total
20: *Number Sense* Working with Place Value; Grouping, Sorting, and Using Patterns; Estimation and Number Sense	1, 2, 3, 7, 31	____/5
21: *Solving Problems* Adding and Subtracting, Multiplying and Dividing, Estimating and Problem Solving	4, 5, 6, 9	____/4
22: *Fractions, Decimals, and Percents* Reading Decimals, Understanding and Comparing Fractions, Understanding Proportion and Percent	10, 11, 12, 13, 14, 15, 16, 17, 18, 19, 20	____/11
23: *Measurements and Formulas* Using English Measurement, Using Metric Measurement, Formulas and Problem Solving	8, 24, 25, 26, 27, 28, 29	____/7
24: *Trends and Predictions: Graphs and Data* Reading Bar, Circle, and Line Graphs; Understanding Spreadsheets; Drawing Conclusions, Seeing Trends, and Finding Averages	21, 22, 23, 30, 32	____/5
	Total	____/32

WHAT YOUR SCORE MEANS

If you got 29–32 correct: You have a strong foundation in the math skills covered in the video programs and workbook. Use the lessons in this workbook to reinforce your skills.

If you got 26–28 correct: You have a basic knowledge of many of the math skills covered in these programs. Work carefully through this workbook to build a strong foundation in workplace math skills.

If you got 22–25 correct: Use the videos and workbook to improve your workplace math skills. By working hard to develop your math skills, you will help prepare yourself for using math in the workplace.

If you got less than 22 correct: You need to learn more about workplace math skills. By watching the video programs and doing the exercises in this book, you can gain the knowledge and skills you need.

Number Sense

OBJECTIVES

In this lesson, you will work with these math concepts and skills to do workplace tasks:

1. Reading and comparing place values
2. Sorting and grouping numbers and using patterns
3. Estimating by using round numbers

Numbers are more common than we often realize. You use them when you are thinking about prices, time, and even your own address. Numbers are used everywhere from home to school to work. Sometimes you must use exact numbers, and at other times you can **estimate,** or find an answer that is close but not exact.

The video program you are about to watch will show you the importance of numbers and how numbers are used in the workplace. It will also show how people organize numbers and how they decide when to estimate.

As you watch the video, think about how you use numbers every day. Notice how often estimation is used. Also watch for situations that require an exact answer instead of an estimate.

Sneak Preview

This exercise previews some of the concepts from Program 20. After you answer the questions, use the Feedback on page 15 to help set your learning goals.

SERVICE: You are working as a customer service representative for a company. The company sells housewares through a mail-order catalog. You just entered a customer's order into the computer. Below is part of the order form that appears on the screen.

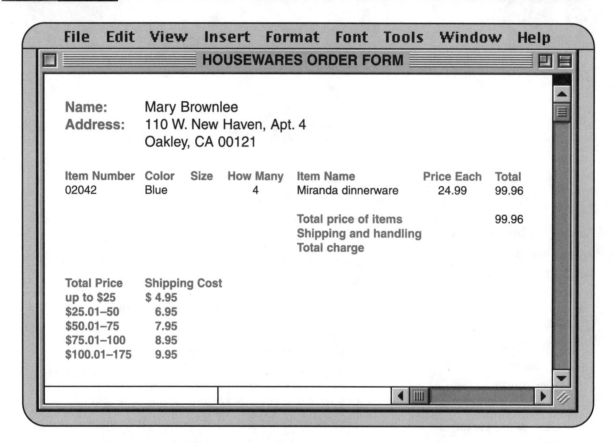

File   Edit   View   Insert   Format   Font   Tools   Window   Help

HOUSEWARES ORDER FORM

Name: Mary Brownlee
Address: 110 W. New Haven, Apt. 4
          Oakley, CA 00121

Item Number	Color	Size	How Many	Item Name	Price Each	Total
02042	Blue		4	Miranda dinnerware	24.99	99.96
				Total price of items		99.96
				Shipping and handling		
				Total charge		

Total Price	Shipping Cost
up to $25	$ 4.95
$25.01–50	6.95
$50.01–75	7.95
$75.01–100	8.95
$100.01–175	9.95

Answer these questions based on the order form.

1. The customer ordered four place settings at $24.99 each. Choose the expression that shows how you could estimate the total price of the items.

   (1) $25 + 4

   (2) $25 - 4

   (3) $25 × 4

   (4) $0.25 + 4

   (5) $0.25 × 4

2. Based on the actual total price of the items that the customer ordered, how much will the customer pay for shipping and handling?

(1) $4.95

(2) $6.95

(3) $7.95

(4) $8.95

(5) $9.95

3. To tell the customer how much she'll pay for this purchase, you should

(1) estimate

(2) find an exact answer

4. List three different pieces of information provided on the order form that are communicated using numbers.

a. _____

b. _____

c. _____

Feedback

- If you got all of the questions right . . .

you have a foundation for working with numbers. Concentrate on how different kinds of numbers are used in the video program.

- If you missed question 1 . . .

you need to work on your estimation skills.

- If you missed question 2 . . .

you need to learn more about the relative size of numbers and how to compare them.

- If you missed question 3 . . .

concentrate on developing your decision-making skills, such as knowing when to estimate and when to use an exact number.

- If you missed question 4 . . .

pay special attention to how numbers are used to communicate in the video and in your daily life.

Answers for Sneak Preview:
1. Choice (3)   **2.** Choice (4)   **3.** Choice (2)   **4.** Any of the following: *address, item number, number ordered, price each, total, total price, or shipping cost.*

Vocabulary for *Number Sense*

alphanumeric	combining letters and numbers, as in a label on items in a store, business, or warehouse
approximate	close, but not exact
bank teller	a person who works directly with customers and their withdrawals from and deposits to the bank
beginning balance	the amount of cash issued to a teller at the beginning of the day
categories	groups based on similarities
compare	to find out which number is larger or smaller
digit	a numeral between 0 and 9
estimate	to find a number that is close but not exact
labels	words used to describe or identify
odometers	instruments that measure distance traveled
place values	the sizes of digits based on their position in a number
range	the values from the lowest number in a group to the highest
round number	a number ending in 0
sort	to put items or numbers in groups based on their similarities or differences
tally	to count and record an amount
teller balancing record	the form a teller uses to account for his or her cash at the end of a business day
working adjustment fund	the difference between a teller's beginning balance and cash at the end of the day

PBS
LiteracyLink®

Now watch Program 20.

After you watch, work on:
- pages 17–32 in this workbook
- Internet activities at www.pbs.org/literacy

AFTER you WATCH

program **20**

Number Sense

WORKTIP

Whenever you use numbers on the job:

- Record them carefully and accurately.
- Use **labels**, such as *feet, dollars, cases,* and so on, whenever needed.
- Use number sense to check whether the numbers you are working with make sense.

On the following pages, you will learn more about the math skills discussed in the video program you just watched. You'll also have the opportunity to practice these skills and others.

Think About the Key Points from the Video Program

Each of these skills is important to developing number sense:

- Reading, writing, comparing, and ordering numbers
- Finding, grouping, and sorting numbers
- Finding patterns in numbers
- Rounding numbers
- Estimating
- Knowing when to estimate and when to use an exact number

The more you work with numbers, the more quickly you will develop these number skills as second nature. As you work through the next fifteen pages, you'll see how large a role number sense plays on the job.

Working with Place Value

Each **digit** in a number has a value, depending on where the digit appears. For example, the 3 in 325 has a different value from the 3 in 13. The 3 in 325 has a **place value** of 300; the 3 in 13 has a place value of just 3.

Because a digit's position in a number determines its place value, it is important to write each digit in its proper place. Imagine that as people pass through a turnstile at a sporting event, a mechanical counter keeps track of the number of people who go through. Look at the counter shown below.

3	6	0	9	5

Reading the digits from left to right, the number on the counter is *thirty-six thousand ninety-five*. Notice that there are no hundreds in 36,095. Instead, the zero is used as a placeholder.

Read each value below, then write it in number form. The first one has been done for you.

1. seven hundred twenty _720_
2. one thousand forty _____
3. seventeen thousand four hundred two _____
4. twenty thousand five hundred sixty _____

Comparing Values

Understanding place value can help you **compare** numbers. Start at the left and look for the first place values that are different. Look at the numbers below.

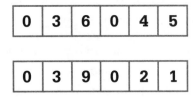

Which of the two numbers is larger? Both numbers have a 0 in the hundred thousands column and a 3 in the ten thousands column. So, compare the digits in the next place value column, the thousands. Because 6 is less than 9, you know that 36,045 is less than 39,021.

Sometimes two number do not have the same number of nonzero digits. Compare these numbers:

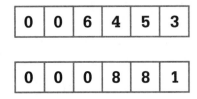

To compare them, start at the left and find the first place where the numbers are different. Compare 6 thousands with 0 thousands. You know that 6 is greater than 0, so you know that 6453 is greater than 881.

Here are the most common symbols for comparing numbers.

COMPARISON SYMBOLS

20 > 8 twenty *is greater than* eight
4 < 12 four *is less than* twelve
9 = 9 nine *equals* nine
7 ≠ 9 seven *does not equal* nine

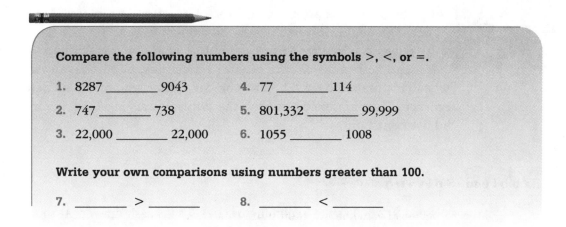

Compare the following numbers using the symbols >, <, or =.

1. 8287 _____ 9043

2. 747 _____ 738

3. 22,000 _____ 22,000

4. 77 _____ 114

5. 801,332 _____ 99,999

6. 1055 _____ 1008

Write your own comparisons using numbers greater than 100.

7. _____ > _____

8. _____ < _____

Ordering Numbers

Putting numbers in order according to size is a useful workplace skill for organizing files, supplies, and so on. Understanding place value will help you put numbers in order—either from smallest to largest, or largest to smallest.

How would the following numbers be ordered from smallest to largest? To compare the numbers, start with the hundreds place.

278   218   191   99

From smallest to largest, the numbers are ordered 99 < 191 < 218 < 278. Notice that 99 has no hundreds, so it is the smallest.

Put these sets of numbers in order from smallest to largest.

1. 38, 33, 41, 101 _____

2. 9, 95, 57, 75 _____

Put these numbers in order from largest to smallest.

3. 1127, 978, 1119, 1125 _____

4. 109, 201, 104, 210 _____

SERVICE: Art Pomero is a **bank teller** at Hillside Bank. In addition to handling cash, Art uses numbers to add and subtract check amounts, look up account balances, and record deposits and withdrawals. To complete many of these tasks, Art uses place value and comparison skills.

On the next page are portions of a **teller balancing record** Art filled out. The **beginning balance** is the amount of cash Hillside issued Art to put in his drawer. At the end of the business day, Art had to **tally** (count) how many of each bill (tens, twenties, hundreds, and so on) was in his cash drawer. Then he compared that amount to his beginning balance. The difference between the two amounts is called a **working adjustment fund.**

Problem Solving

Art was issued $12,500 as the beginning balance for his cash drawer. At the end of the day, he tallied the following amount in his drawer:

100s 57 bills	**50s** 7 bills	**20s** 100 bills
10s 45 bills	**5s** 100 bills	**1s** 33 bills

Fill out the teller banking record on the next page. The following directions tell you how to fill it in:

1. First, fill in the shaded area labeled ADJUSTMENTS. Using the tally above, write in the total dollar amount of each type of bill. The 100s have been done for you. Since Art has 57 one-hundred dollar bills, he has $5700.

2. Add up all of the amounts listed under ADJUSTMENTS. This is the total amount in your cash drawer at the end of the day. Write that amount next to TOTAL.

3. Take the amount you wrote next to TOTAL and write that number next to Ending Balance on the top left of the teller balancing record. Also fill in the Beginning Balance space with the amount Art started with in his cash drawer (from page 20).

4. Subtract to find the difference between the beginning balance and the end balance. Write this amount next to Working Fund Adj. (Adj. means adjustment.) This amount shows how much more or less Art has in his cash drawer than he started with. At the end of this day, he has less than the amount he started with. You write a total like this with <brackets>, such as <$100>.

5. Write the working fund adjustment amount in the correct place on the right side of the form. Subtract this amount from the Total Checks for Deposits amount, which has been filled in. Write this new amount in the space labeled Net Cash—Net.

Teller Balancing Record

Date _____

Ending Balance		
Beginning Balance		
Took to Vault		
Got from Vault		
Working Fund Adj.		

Total Checks for Deposits	14,421	21
Total Checks Disbursed		
Cash Over		
Cash Short		
Working Fund Adj.		
Net Cash-Net		
ADJUSTMENTS		
Marked Money		
100s	5,700	00
50s		
20s		
10s		
5s		
1s		
TOTAL		

Congratulations! You have just filled out a Teller Balancing Record similar to one that bank tellers use when they close out at the end of the day.

COMMUNICATE

In today's world, a lot of information about people is communicated through numbers. You can tell someone how to reach you by giving your telephone number. The government keeps track of your wages and taxes using Social Security numbers. Your bank identifies you by your account number.

In three minutes, tell someone about yourself using as many different numbers as possible. Or write down some information about yourself using the numbers in your life.

Grouping, Sorting, and Using Patterns

The numbers we use in life and on the job appear in many different places—on paycheck stubs, signs, and even drawings. Most times, numbers appear with labels—either right next to the number or as a heading in a chart or graph. These labels help you work with numbers.

The information below appears in an employee handbook at a binder manufacturer. Each number has a label such as *shift, hours, labels,* and *minutes* to identify the number. Look at the labels used with each number. How many hours does an employee spend inspecting binders in an 8-hour shift?

- 1 shift = 8 hours
- Six employees should be working each shift.
- There are two shifts operating each workday.
- In $3\frac{1}{2}$ hours, each employee is expected to apply 175 tags.
- Each lunch break is 30 minutes.
- During the last 4 hours of the shift, employee inspects 225 binders.

Each employee inspects binders for the last **4 hours** of each shift.

Use the information above to answer these questions. Include labels with your answers.

1. How much time does an employee have to apply 175 tags? _____

2. If you subtract the amount of time for lunch, how long does an employee work in one shift? (1 hr. = 60 min.) _____

3. How many employees should work each shift? _____

4. How many shifts are worked in five workdays? _____

Sorting and Grouping Numbers

To use numbers effectively, we often need to put them into **categories,** or groups. We **sort** and group numbers based on their similarities (what is the same) and differences (what is different).

Look at the information below. It describes the mesh screens being packed in a shipping department.

Part #VQ901: 32 inches wide; 4 feet tall; $\frac{3}{4}$-inch gauge

Part #VQ934: 40 inches wide; $5\frac{1}{2}$ feet tall; $\frac{3}{4}$-inch gauge

Part #VQ022: 42 inches wide; 6 feet tall; $\frac{1}{2}$-inch gauge

Part #VQ121: 48 inches wide; 5 feet tall; $\frac{1}{2}$-inch gauge

Part #VQ207: 48 inches wide; 6 feet tall; $\frac{3}{4}$-inch gauge

Which parts could be grouped as $\frac{3}{4}$-inch gauge screens? You're right if you grouped parts **VQ901, VQ934,** and **VQ207** together. They are all the same gauge: $\frac{3}{4}$ inch.

> **Use the information on page 22 to sort these screens. Write the appropriate part number.**
>
> 1. **a.** screens under 6 feet tall: _____
>   **b.** screens 6 feet tall and over: _____
>
> 2. **a.** 48-inch-wide screens: _____
>   **b.** screens that are not 48 inches wide: _____
>
> 3. **a.** $\frac{1}{2}$-inch gauge screens: _____
>   **b.** screens that are greater than $\frac{1}{2}$-inch gauge: _____
>
> 4. **a.** screens less than 42 inches wide: _____
>   **b.** screens 42 inches wide or greater: _____

Using Patterns

Sometimes when you work with numbers, you may see a pattern developing. A number pattern is a sequence of numbers that repeats itself or follows a rule. Let's take a look at a number pattern that is common in the workplace. Do you see the pattern in the chart below?

number of shifts	1	2	3		5	6
hours worked	4	8		16	20	
wage earned	$35	$70	$105	$140	$	$210

The chart shows that one shift is equal to 4 hours. Multiplying the number of shifts by 4 will tell you the total hours worked. Also, if you multiply the number of shifts by $35, you will get the total wages earned.

> **Use the chart above to answer these questions. Assume that this number pattern continues beyond the information given in the chart.**
>
> 1. How many shifts are equal to 16 hours? _____
> 2. To earn $105, how many hours would you have to work? _____
> 3. How much would you earn if you worked 5 shifts? _____
> 4. How many hours are there in 6 shifts? _____
> 5. How many shifts would you have to work to earn $280? _____
> 6. How much money would you earn in a 40-hour week? _____

MANUFACTURING: Alicia James works in the shipping and receiving department of a furniture company, where she does quite a bit of sorting and grouping. Not only does she sort by item (for example, all chairs in one area and all beds in another), but she uses identification numbers to record and group its many items. Alicia therefore must be able to read, compare, sort, and group numbers quickly and accurately.

On the next page you will find a receiving inventory form Alicia received along with a shipment of materials. It lists the items that were in the shipment, their identification numbers, and where they are to be stored.

Below is a map of the warehouse. The map indicates the different storage areas at Alicia's company. For example, Area A houses all items identified by the **alphanumeric** label "WW900." If an item with this label is received into the warehouse, it should be stored in Area A.

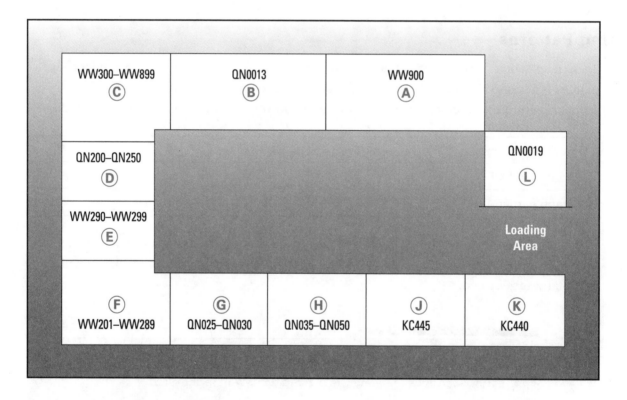

Problem Solving

As a warehouse worker, Alicia needs to make sure that the items on the receiving inventory form are stored where they should be. She therefore must record the storage area to be used for each item.

Fill in the letter on the form for items 2 through 4. The first one is done for you.

To find the correct storage area for items 5 through 10, Alicia must understand **range.** Storage Areas C, D, E, and F contain more than one item type. Each of these areas stores items that range from one identification number to another. For example, Area C contains all items that have an identification number that lies between WW300 and WW899, including those two numbers.

Would you find item #WW488 in Area C? Yes, you would, because 488 is greater than 300 and less than 899.

$$300 < 488 < 899$$

Would #WW299 be stored in Area C? No, because 299 is less than the lowest number in the Area C range.

Fill out the inventory receiving form for items 5 through 10.

Date: _____   Shipment #: 9804481

	ITEM #	RECEIVED	STORAGE AREA
1.	KC445	✓	J
2.	QN0013	✓	
3.	WW900	✓	
4.	KC440	✓	
5.	WW898	✓	
6.	QN026	✓	
7.	QN040	✓	
8.	WW389	✓	
9.	QN049	✓	
10.	QN200	✓	

NuCom
WAREHOUSE
16 Sheldon Highway

WRITE IT

Patterns exist everywhere, not just in numbers. For example, stripes are a *visual pattern*. There are *auditory* patterns in music. As you learned in this lesson, a pattern is a sequence that repeats itself or follows a rule.

Take out a notebook, and describe a pattern that you are familiar with. Use detailed words to tell exactly what the pattern is and where it is found. If you are stuck without an idea, look at this book. What can you say about all of the left-hand page numbers?

Estimation and Number Sense

You saw on the videotape how often people estimate on the job. When you **estimate,** you find numbers that are **approximate**—that is, close but not exact. The language of estimating often includes phrases such as *just about, close to, almost,* and *around.* For example, if it takes you 62 minutes to get to work, you might say that it takes "about an hour."

When you estimate, you often use round numbers. A **round number** is a number that is close to your original number and ends in zero. What round number is 38 close to?

30 < 38 < 40   *You know that 38 is between two round numbers—30 and 40. You can use your number sense to figure out that 38 is closer to 40 than to 30. We can say that 38 **rounds up** to 40.*

What happens when a number is exactly halfway between two round numbers? In this case, people usually round up to the higher number.

10 < 15 < 20   *15 is not closer to either 10 or 20. In this case, round up. 15 rounds to 20.*

Round each number to a number to the nearest ten.

1. 133 rounds to _____

2.   7 rounds to _____

3. 11 rounds to _____

4. 46 rounds to _____

5.   27 rounds to _____

6. 255 rounds to _____

7.   96 rounds to _____

8.   35 rounds to _____

Estimating with Easy Numbers

When you do not need an exact answer, you can get a good estimate by using numbers that are easy to work with. Round numbers are easy to work with. How would you use round numbers to estimate an answer to this problem?

58 pairs of rubber gloves + 23 pairs of rubber gloves = ?

To find an *exact* answer, you know that you'd add 58 and 23. But if you only need an *estimate* of the number of rubber gloves, you can use numbers that are much easier to work with.

58 rounds to 60, and 23 rounds to 20

60 + 20 = 80

There are *approximately* 80 pairs of rubber gloves. The symbol we use to indicate *approximately equal to* is $\approx$, so $58 + 23 \approx 80$.

See page 147 in the Reference Handbook for more examples of rounding.

Estimate an answer for each of the following problems. Show the numbers you are rounding to. The first one is done for you.

1. 597 workers ÷ 29 office sites = about _____ workers per site

   600 ÷ 30 = 20 workers per site

2. 72 rods + 101 rods + 13 rods = approximately _____ rods

3. 33 minutes × 11 days = approximately _____ minutes

4. $153 − $41 = about $_____

5. 204 inches ÷ 12 inches = about _____ inches

Estimating with Money

When you have a dollar bill, three quarters, and two dimes in your pocket, you say that you have "about two dollars." Estimating with money is very much like rounding other numbers. Most often, any amount that is fifty cents or over is rounded up to the next dollar. Any amount less than fifty cents is rounded down.

$14.27 rounds to $14 because 27 cents is less than 50 cents (27 < 50).

$109.68 rounds to $110 because 68 cents is greater than 50 cents (68 > 50).

Round each amount to the nearest dollar.

1. $16.74 rounds to _____

2. $987.14 rounds to _____

3. $25.01 rounds to _____

4. $12.49 rounds to _____

5. $101.50 rounds to _____

6. $9.70 rounds to _____

7. $802.32 rounds to _____

8. $1020.57 rounds to _____

CONSTRUCTION: Cliff Pearson is a worker on a construction site. He works with numbers when he reads schedules, orders and purchases materials, and measures. Sometimes Cliff does math that involves finding exact figures, but at other times, a rough estimate is enough.

Cliff needs to buy a ladder, so he studies the advertisement for ladders shown below. These ladders come in different heights, types, and materials, and their prices vary. Deciding which ladder to buy depends upon who will be using the ladder and for what purpose.

HOW TO CHOOSE A LADDER	**WHAT IS DUTY RATING?** Duty rating is your weight plus the weight of the tools and materials you carry up a ladder.	
TYPE III • For general light-duty household use • 200 lb. duty rating	**WOOD STEP TYPE III** 2' $ 9.99 4' $ 18.77 6' $ 21.00	**ALUMINUM EXTENSION TYPE III** 16' $ 47.00 20' $ 77.00 24' $104.00
TYPE II • For medium commercial use, like painting or light maintenance work • 225 lb. duty rating	**FIBERGLASS STEP TYPE I** 4' $ 54.00 6' $ 62.00 8' $ 96.00	**ALUMINUM EXTENSION TYPE II** 20' $106.00 24' $125.00 28' $159.00
TYPE I • For heavy-duty industrial use • 250 lb. duty rating		
PRO QUALITY TYPE IA • For extra-heavy-duty industrial use • Fiberglass ladders perfect for use around electrical wire • Extra-heavy-duty 300 lb. duty rating	**FIBERGLASS STEP TYPE IA** 6' $ 77.00 8' $114.00	**ALUMINUM EXTENSION TYPE I** 28' $198.00 32' $236.00 40' $282.00

Problem Solving

To decide what ladder to buy, construction workers usually pay attention to three numbers:

- What *height* ladder do I need? Ladder height is usually given in feet, and the symbol ' is often used to mean *feet*: 6' = 6 feet.
- What *duty rating* should I look for? Duty rating is equal to the weight of the person using the ladder plus the weight of the tools and materials he or she will carry up the ladder.
- What is the *price*?

Answering these questions rarely requires finding exact numbers. Instead, rough estimates of height, weight, and price are enough to make a good decision and get the job done. Use the advertisement on page 28 to answer the following questions.

Estimate the cost of the items below. Round each amount to the nearest $10. The first one is done for you.

1. a 4-foot wood stepladder, type III $18.77 \approx $20.00

2. a 16-foot aluminum extension ladder, type III $ _____

3. a 40-foot aluminum extension ladder, type I $ _____

4. an 8-foot fiberglass stepladder, type IA $ _____

5. a 20-foot aluminum extension ladder, type II $ _____

Answer the following questions.

6. Bernice weighs 155 pounds. She needs a six-foot ladder. All she will carry up the ladder are a gallon of paint, a brush, and a scraper, totaling less than 5 pounds. She does not want to pay more than $25. What is the least expensive ladder she should use?_____

7. A foreman on a construction site needs a ladder to climb about 27 feet to do some roofing work. The workers on the site weigh between 190 and 220 pounds each. In addition, roof shingles and tools for the job weigh close to 20 pounds. What is the least expensive ladder the foreman should choose?_____

8. Angelo just accepted the job of replacing gutters on a school building. He needs a ladder that extends to at least 27 feet. Angelo weighs 185 pounds and carries a 10-pound tool belt. In addition, he'll sometimes need to carry up to 15 pounds of gutter up the ladder. What is the least expensive ladder he should use?

_____

READ IT ....

Advertisements are used on billboards, on television, in newspapers, and in magazines to try to catch our eye. Usually, an advertisement is trying to sell something. What do you think makes a good advertisement? Why do you think advertising works?

Circle the numbers you see in three different advertisements. Notice the kinds of words, phrases, and numbers used. Why do you think so many prices end in the number 99?

Review

Below is a shipping invoice from a grocery warehouse. It shows how much of a product was ordered, how much was actually shipped, the product code, and how much the item cost.

Jane B. Davidson, Inc.
QUALITY PRODUCE
"fresh and flavorful"

16 Spring Street, Boston, MA 02114

Date _____

Invoice # _____

Page _____

Bill to: Anderson Supermarkets
(800) 888-8888

Ship to: Anderson/Jamestown
1135 Morey Blvd.
Sandton, MA 00000

Quantity Ordered (cases)	Quantity Shipped (cases)	Product Code	Description	Price/Each Case	Total Amount
4	4	1020	Cortland apples	$21.25	$85.00
2	2	1200	Red Delicious	$19.25	$38.50
10	10	1260	Granny Smith	$26.75	$267.50
2	0	1280	Golden Delicious	0.00	0.00
1	1	3020	Papayas	$15.75	$15.75
3	0	3030	Pineapple	0.00	0.00
5	5	5300	Zucchini squash	$8.25	$41.25
4	4	5340	Butternut squash	$9.75	$39.00
1	1	5390	Buttercup squash	$9.75	$9.75
1	1	6210	Carrot shredded	$9.25	$9.25
1	1	6310	Celery sticks	$9.00	$9.00
1	1	6350	Romano salad	$11.25	$11.25
5	5	2100	Oranges	$36.25	$181.25
1	1	2410	Avocados	$47.75	$47.75
20	20	2440	Nectarines	$21.25	$425.00
2	2	2450	Bartlett pears	$25.75	$51.50
2	0	2480	Fresh figs	0.00	0.00

Use the grocery store invoice on page 30 and the number skills you've worked on in this program to answer the following questions.

1. Write the product code number for each item below.

   a. Red Delicious apples _____

   b. oranges _____

   c. butternut squash _____

   d. fresh figs _____

2. List the products that the store owners ordered more than 4 cases of:

   _____

   _____

   _____

3. Put the following products in order of price per case, from least expensive to most expensive:

   Granny Smith apples, celery sticks, romano salad, oranges, Bartlett pears, and papayas

   least expensive: _____

   _____

   _____

   _____

   _____

   most expensive: _____

4. Use the product codes and the guide below to find where the following items are stored.

Product Code	Location
1000–2000	Storage Area A
2100–2900	Refrigeration Unit #1
3000–4900	Refrigeration Unit #2
5000–6200	Storage Area B
6201–7000	Storage Area C

   a. shredded carrots _____

   b. pineapple _____

   c. nectarines _____

   d. Golden Delicious apples _____

5. At Anderson Supermarket, one of your responsibilities is to review and sign the shipping invoice. You always estimate the total amount as a way of quickly checking the numbers. As a first step, estimate the total amount for each product by rounding the price for each case to the nearest ten dollars multiplying by the quantity shipped.

Description	Quantity Shipped (cases)	Price/Each Case	Estimated Total Amount
Cortland apples	4	$21.25	
Red Delicious	2	$19.25	
Granny Smith	10	$26.75	
Golden Delicious	0	0.00	
Papayas	1	$15.75	
Pineapple	0	0.00	
Zucchini squash	5	$8.25	
Butternut squash	4	$9.75	
Buttercup squash	1	$9.75	
Carrot shredded	1	$9.25	
Celery sticks	1	$9.00	
Romano salad	1	$11.25	
Oranges	5	$36.25	
Avocados	1	$47.75	
Nectarines	20	$21.25	
Bartlett pears	2	$25.75	
Fresh figs	0	0.00	

Solving Problems

OBJECTIVES

In this lesson, you will
work with the following
math concepts and skills
to do workplace tasks:

1. Adding and
   subtracting numbers
2. Multiplying and
   dividing numbers
3. Estimating with
   lead digits and
   compatible pairs,
   and to check
   work done with
   a calculator

The video program you are about to watch will show
how and when people do math **calculations** on the
job. You'll see people adding, subtracting, multiplying,
and dividing. You'll see them working with pencil and
paper, as well as with calculators.

As you watch the video, notice the strategies that people
use to get answers and check that their answers make
sense. It's a good idea to develop such strategies, because
we all make mistakes now and then. Problem-solving
strategies will help you prevent many mistakes and
correct the ones that do occur.

The best way to learn basic skills in math is through lots
of practice. The more you practice adding, subtracting,
multiplying, and dividing, the more number sense you'll
develop. You can also enhance your number sense by
estimating with these basic skills.

Sneak Preview

This exercise previews some of the concepts from Program 21. After you answer the questions, use the Feedback on page 35 to help set your learning goals.

MANUFACTURING: You are working as an assistant in the personnel office of a large factory. One of your jobs is to figure out how many hours each shift has worked on a daily, weekly, and monthly basis. The form below lists each employee's hours for one week.

Employee and Shift Number	Mon.	Tues.	Wed.	Thurs.	Fri.
William Antiago (Shift #1)	9	9	9	9	0
Joyce Azzoni (Shift #3)	8	8	8	8	8
Wayne Carleton (Shift #2)	7	7	7	8	8
Bradley Deghan (Shift #2)	6	7	8	9	8
Vera Delgado (Shift #2)	8	8	8	0	8
Nancy Finch (Shift #1)	5	5	5	6	6
Peter Grace (Shift #3)	0	0	9	9	9
Manuel Hanson (Shift #1)	8	9	9	7	9
Tyrone Larson (Shift #2)	8	8	8	8	9
Catherine Nyhan (Shift #3)	0	7	7	7	7
Nick Pochet (Shift #1)	4	4	4	5	4
Sheila Slade (Shift #3)	6	6	6	0	0
Max Wilson (Shift #1)	8	8	8	8	8
Michael Zerfas (Shift #1)	9	9	9	8	8
TOTAL					

1. Estimate the total number of hours worked by William Antiago by rounding to the nearest ten.

   (1) 10   **(4)** 40
   (2) 20   **(5)** 50
   (3) 30

2. Shift #2 employees worked a total of 148 hours this week. Divide this number by 4 to find the average hours worked per employee.

   (1) 32   **(4)** 40
   (2) 30   **(5)** 37
   (3) 35

3. Peter Grace earns $5.80 per hour. How much money did he earn this week?

   (1) $156.60   **(4)** $40.60
   (2) $116.00   **(5)** $52.20
   (3) $540.50

4. How many more hours were worked by all shifts on Thursday than on Monday?

   (1) 92   **(4)** 86
   (2) 178   **(5)** 12
   (3) 6

Feedback

- If you got all of the questions right . . .   your basic operation skills are good. Concentrate on the kinds of problem solving shown in the video.

- If you missed question 1 . . .   you need to work on your estimation skills.

- If you missed question 2 . . .   you need to work on your division skills.

- If you missed question 3 . . .   you need to work on your multiplication skills.

- If you missed question 4 . . .   you need to work on your ability to decide *how* to solve a problem.

Answers for Sneak Preview:
1. Choice (4) 2. Choice (5) 3. Choice (1) 4. Choice (3)

Vocabulary for *Solving Problems*

area	the size of a surface
calculations	math processes—such as adding, subtracting, multiplying, and dividing—carried out to solve a problem
compatible pairs	sets of two numbers that divide equally
decimal point	the point that separates whole numbers from parts of a whole or dollars from cents
difference	the result when one number is subtracted from another
dividend	the number being divided up in a division problem; the number inside the long division sign
front-end estimation	a method of estimating with large numbers by using only the first digits of the numbers
lead digits	the first (left) digits of numbers
products	the results when two or more numbers are multiplied together
quotient	the result when one number is divided by another
reconciliation sheet	a form that a store uses to record the flow of money at a cash register
regroup	to move an amount to or from a place value to complete a basic operation
remainder	the amount left after dividing two numbers that do not divide evenly; for example, $5 \div 2$ is 2 with a remainder of 1
square units	labels that express size in two dimensions (length and width)
sum	the result when two or more numbers are added together

PBS LiteracyLink®

Now watch Program 21.

After you watch, work on:
- pages 37–52 in this workbook
- Internet activities at www.pbs.org/literacy

AFTER you WATCH

Solving Problems

WORKTIP

Adding, subtracting, multiplying, and dividing numbers on the job can be easier if you:

- Work carefully and accurately.
- Remember basic number facts.
- Use a calculator when possible.
- Check your work when finished.

On the following pages, you will learn more about how to perform basic math operations. You'll use pencil and paper to find answers most of the time, and you'll have a chance to use a calculator to check your work. You'll also get some practice estimating.

Think About the Key Points from the Video Program

- Addition and subtraction are used on the job all the time. Many jobs involve adding and subtracting money amounts; these skills are especially important.

- Multiplying and dividing numbers solves many problems on the job. If you are working with money, you need to know where to place the **decimal point** when you multiply or divide.

- Estimating can save time and therefore money. To succeed with numbers on the job, you must know when estimation is appropriate.

- Calculators are extremely helpful tools. To use them successfully, be careful to input numbers correctly.

Adding and Subtracting

You know that adding is putting amounts together and subtracting is taking an amount away from another, or finding a **difference.** When you add or subtract using paper and pencil, you must *line the digits up correctly*—ones under ones, tens under tens, hundreds under hundreds, and so on. When you solve the problem 1240 + 145, line up digits like this:

$$
\begin{array}{r}
1240 \\
+\ \ 145 \\
\hline
\end{array}
\qquad \text{NOT THIS:} \qquad
\begin{array}{r}
1240 \\
+\ 145 \\
\hline
\end{array}
$$

And when you subtract eight hundred thirteen from one thousand nine hundred eighty-five, the problem should look like this:

$$
\begin{array}{r}
1985 \\
-\ \ 813 \\
\hline
\end{array}
\qquad \text{NOT THIS:} \qquad
\begin{array}{r}
1985 \\
-\ 813 \\
\hline
\end{array}
$$

Once the problem is lined up correctly, start at the right column and move left, adding or subtracting each digit.

$$
\begin{array}{r}
1240 \\
+\ \ 145 \\
\hline
1385
\end{array}
\qquad\qquad
\begin{array}{r}
1985 \\
-\ \ 813 \\
\hline
1172
\end{array}
$$

Solve these problems on a separate sheet of paper. Be sure to line up the digits correctly.

1. 9546 − 7321 = _____
2. 1280 + 413 = _____
3. 67 + 21 = _____
4. 89,488 − 135 = _____
5. 823 + 46 = _____
6. 944 − 12 = _____
7. 1582 − 371 = _____
8. 647 + 22 = _____

Adding and Subtracting with Regrouping

When you add digits in a place value column, their **sum** may be 10 or more. When this happens, an amount will have to be carried, or **regrouped,** to the next place value.

$$
\begin{array}{r}
^{1\ 1} \\
688 \\
+\ \ 59 \\
\hline
747
\end{array}
$$

8 + 9 = 17, so put a 7 in the ones place and regroup the 1 to the tens place. Since 1 + 8 + 5 = 14, put a 4 in the tens place and regroup the 1 to the hundreds place.

You may also have to regroup when you subtract. If you are subtracting a larger digit from a smaller one, regroup by borrowing. Regrouping does not change the number's value.

$$
\begin{array}{r}
\overset{\scriptsize 1\ 11\ 1}{\cancel{2}\cancel{2}5} \\
-\ \ 29 \\
\hline
196
\end{array}
$$

You cannot take 9 from 5, so regroup 1 ten from the tens place. 15 − 9 = 6, so put a 6 in the ones column. Since you cannot subtract 2 from the 1 left in the tens place, regroup 1 from the hundreds place. 11 − 2 = 9, so put a 9 in the tens place. Bring down the 1 left in the hundreds place, since nothing is being subtracted from it.

For help with subtracting from zeros, turn to Reference Handbook page 145.

Solve these problems on a separate sheet of paper. Regroup when necessary. Be sure to line the digits up correctly.

1. 2017 − 345 = _____
2. 8380 − 298 = _____
3. 229 + 984 = _____
4. 458 + 275 = _____
5. 1409 + 11 = _____
6. 1950 − 160 = _____

Adding and Subtracting Money

Adding and subtracting money is like working with whole numbers except that you need to remember where the decimal point goes. When you line up the digits, be sure to line up the decimal points, one under the other.

To add $435.98 to $112.03, line up the decimal points and add.

decimal points lined up

$$
\begin{array}{r}
\$112.03 \\
+\ \ \ 435.98 \\
\hline
\$548.01
\end{array}
$$

To subtract $47.52 from $358.90, line up the decimal points and subtract.

decimal points lined up

$$
\begin{array}{r}
\$358.90 \\
-\ \ \ 47.52 \\
\hline
\$311.38
\end{array}
$$

Add or subtract these money amounts on a separate piece of paper. Be careful to line up the decimal points correctly.

1. $879.65 − $402.87 = _____
2. $2870.45 + $1590.23 = _____
3. $245.75 − $95.09 = _____
4. $675.50 + $250.75 = _____
5. $342.68 − $24.89 = _____
6. $4128.14 + $670.29 = _____
7. $905.62 − $796.54 = _____
8. $290.86 + $824.81 = _____

SERVICE: As a restaurant server, Rosalie Chen works hard to make sure that her customers have a pleasant experience. She is responsible for writing down orders, answering customer questions about the menu, and collecting proper payment at the end of the meal. Rosalie's pleasant personality and good communication skills are very important to her success in her job at Danita's Diner.

Rosalie also needs good math skills. Servers sometimes use a calculator, but like many servers, Rosalie must add and subtract with paper and pencil. She has to work carefully so that the bill and the amount of change back are accurate.

Below is a menu from Danita's Diner. Rosalie's first four tables placed the orders shown in the guest checks on the next page.

Problem Solving

Use the menu prices to fill in the correct amount for each item ordered. Then add up all the amounts, and write the total due in the space provided. Finally, figure out the change back if each customer paid with a $20 bill.

DANITA'S DINER

SPECIAL VALUES

3 x 3: 3 eggs, 3 slices toast,
3 slices bacon...............$3.95

2 timer: 2 eggs and 2 slices
bacon..............................$2.95

EGGS

1 egg any style/toast........$1.05
2 eggs any style/toast.......$1.95
3 eggs any style/toast.......$2.95

eggs benedict $3.25

omelette: plain $2.45
with cheese...................$2.75
mushroom & cheese $3.05

PANCAKES, ETC.

regular pancakes $2.45
tall stack $2.95

pancake platter
with side bacon $3.95

waffle: plain......................$2.15
with strawberries..........$2.75

muffin...................................$.90

bagel: plain ....$.80
with cream cheese.......$1.15

French toast.......................$2.15

SIDE ORDERS

bacon $1.45
sausage $1.55
ham.......................................$1.55

hash browns.......................$1.05

cold cereal ....$.95

fruit plate $2.05

BEVERAGES

coffee.....................................$.75
tea..$.65
milk ....$.95

orange juice: small..............$.85
large...............................$1.15

Check No. 4507

Server: _____ Date: _____

eggs benedict	_____
side bacon	_____
2 eggs over easy / toast	_____
lg. orange juice	_____
2 coffees	_____
TOTAL DUE	_____

Change back from $20: _____

Check No. 4508

Server: _____ Date: _____

side sausage	_____
pancake platter	_____
2 muffins	_____
bagel/cream cheese	_____
sm orange juice	_____
waffle w/strawberries	_____
2 sides bacon	_____
1 milk	_____
3 coffees	_____
1 tea	_____
TOTAL DUE	_____

Change back from $20: _____

Check No. 4509

Server: _____ Date: _____

3 eggs scrambled/toast	_____
ham	_____
mushroom/cheese omelet	_____
lg. orange juice	_____
cold cereal	_____
fruit plate	_____
4 coffees	_____
TOTAL DUE	_____

Change back from $20: _____

Check No. 4510

Server: _____ Date: _____

3 X 3 Special	_____
pancakes	_____
French toast	_____
bagel/butter	_____
2 soft-boiled eggs/toast	_____
2 sides bacon	_____
1 coffee	_____
2 teas	_____
2 milks	_____
TOTAL DUE	_____

Change back from $20: _____

COMMUNICATE

Pair up with a classmate or friend. Using the menu above, take turns having one person give an order and the other person take down orders as if you were a customer and a restaurant server. Add up the total of each order you take.

Multiplying and Dividing

Whether you're estimating or calculating exact amounts, it is vital that you know the basic number facts. If you do not know the basic multiplication facts by heart, practice them until you can recall them automatically.

After you know the multiplication facts, you can move on to more challenging calculations. Multiplying two-digit numbers involves just three processes: 1) using basic multiplication facts, 2) regrouping just as you did with addition, and 3) adding **products** together to find a total. To multiply 43 by 72, follow the steps below.

STEP 1

$$\begin{array}{r} 43 \\ \times\ 72 \\ \hline 86 \end{array}$$

$2 \times 3 = 6$
$2 \times 4 = 8$

STEP 2

$$\begin{array}{r} \overset{2}{4}3 \\ \times\ 72 \\ \hline 86 \\ 301 \end{array}$$

$7 \times 3 = 21$, so put 1 in the tens place, and carry the 2.
$7 \times 4 = 28$. Add the 2 to get 30.

STEP 3

$$\begin{array}{r} 43 \\ \times\ 72 \\ \hline 86 \\ 301 \\ \hline \mathbf{3096} \end{array}$$

Add the products.

Notice in Step 2 that when you are multiplying the top number by the 7 in the tens place, the last digit of the product is written *in the tens place.* That's because you're really multiplying by 70. Similarly, when you multiply by a digit in the hundreds place, the product ends in the hundreds place, and so on.

> **Multiply the following numbers on a separate sheet of paper. Put the larger number on the top to make your work easier.**
>
> 1. $21 \times 4 =$ _____
> 2. $63 \times 6 =$ _____
> 3. $65 \times 95 =$ _____
> 4. $15 \times 49 =$ _____
> 5. $223 \times 41 =$ _____
> 6. $78 \times 325 =$ _____

Dividing

When you divide, work from left to right. Notice the placement of each digit in the solution to $496 \div 8$.

STEP 1

$$\begin{array}{r} 6 \\ 8\overline{)496} \\ 48 \\ \hline 1 \end{array}$$

← Divide: 8 goes into 49 six times.
← Write the product: $8 \times 6 = 48$.
← Subtract: 49 minus 48 equals 1.

STEP 2

$$\begin{array}{r} 62 \\ 8\overline{)496} \\ 48 \\ \hline 16 \\ 16 \\ \hline 0 \end{array}$$

Bring down the 6.
Divide: 8 goes into 16 two times.
← Write the product: $2 \times 8 = 16$.
← Subtract: 16 minus 16 equals 0. There is no **remainder.**

Dividing by a number with more than 1 digit involves the same steps, but the numbers you are working with may be more challenging. To solve $300 \div 12$, follow the steps below.

STEP 1

$$12\overline{)300}$$ quotient 2, 24, 6

12 goes into 30 two times with 6 remaining.

STEP 2

$$12\overline{)300}$$ quotient 25, 24, 60, 60, 0

Bring down the 0. 12 goes into 60 five times with no remainder.

Divide the following numbers on a separate sheet of paper. Set up the problem so that the number being divided is *inside* the division bracket.

1. $224 \div 16 =$ _____
2. $3220 \div 20 =$ _____
3. $410 \div 5 =$ _____
4. $3285 \div 9 =$ _____
5. $720 \div 24 =$ _____
6. $3876 \div 34 =$ _____

Multiplying and Dividing with Money

Multiplying and dividing with money is almost the same as working with whole numbers. However, you must decide where to place the decimal point.

When you multiply, add the number of digits that come after the decimal point in both numbers. That is the number of digits that should follow the decimal point in your answer. Take a look:

$$\begin{array}{r} \$1.39 \\ \times\ \ 12 \\ \hline 2\,78 \\ 13\,9 \\ \hline \$16.68 \end{array}$$

2 decimal places following the decimal point
0 decimal places

2 + 0 = 2 decimal places

When you divide a decimal by a whole number, place the decimal point in your answer directly above the decimal point in the **dividend.** (The dividend is the number being divided.)

$$\begin{array}{r} \$\ 4.65 \\ 4\overline{)\$18.60} \\ 16 \\ \hline 2\,6 \\ 2\,4 \\ \hline 20 \\ 20 \\ \hline 0 \end{array}$$

The decimal point in $4.65 is directly above the decimal point in $18.60.

Multiply or divide as indicated.

1. $\$5.87 \times 24 =$ _____
2. $35 \times \$8.80 =$ _____
3. $\$205.45 \div 5 =$ _____
4. $\$603.50 \div 17 =$ _____
5. $\$14.15 \times 25 =$ _____
6. $\$60.95 \div 5 =$ _____

CONSTRUCTION: As a tile worker, Celia McClintock takes measurements of floors and walls to be tiled, buys materials, and lays the tile. Many of these tasks require basic math operations.

For example, some jobs require that Celia multiply the lengths and widths of a kitchen to find the number of square feet in the room. Or she may have to add the costs of materials and labor to get the total amount. Whatever the math operation, she often checks her work by using a calculator as well as paper and pencil.

The worksheet on the next page summarizes several of Celia's jobs. To complete these jobs, Celia will have to make a trip to the tile warehouse to pick up materials. She wants to do all measuring and math operations correctly to avoid buying too much or having to go back for more materials.

Problem Solving

To figure out how much tile to buy, Celia needs to know the **area** of the space to be tiled, that is, the amount of flat surface to be covered. To find the area of a rectangular surface, you multiply the width of the surface by its length. The formula used to express this relationship is:

$$\text{area} \rightarrow A = l \times w \leftarrow \text{width}$$
$$\uparrow$$
$$\text{length}$$

Therefore, if a room measures 25 feet long and 12 feet wide, you find the area of this room by inserting these values into the area formula:

$A = l \times w$
$A = 25 \text{ feet} \times 12 \text{ feet}$
$A = 300 \text{ square feet}$

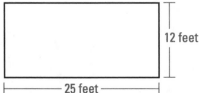

Area is given in **square units.** A square foot measures 1 foot in length and 1 foot in width as shown below.

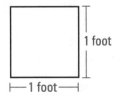

Complete Celia's worksheet below using the following directions. The
121 Larks St. job is filled in for you. Use a calculator if you wish.

1. In Column C, write the amount of tile needed for each job on the tile list
    (length multiplied by width).

    Example: Press: Calculator Displays:

    | 8 | 8. |
    | × | 8. |
    | 9 | 9. |
    | = | 72. |

2. In column E, write the number of cases of tile needed for each job. One case of
    tile covers eleven square feet. (Note: If there is a remainder when you divide,
    always order another full case.)

    Example: Press: Calculator Displays:

    | 7 | 2 | 72. | *number of square feet of tile needed* |
    | ÷ | 72. | |
    | 1 | 1 | 11. | *number of square feet covered per case* |
    | = | 6.545454545 | *number of cases needed* |

    You need to order **7 cases.**

A	B	C	D	E
Job	**Room Measurements** (length × width)	**Tile Needed**	**Type/Cost of Tile** (per sq. ft.)	**Number of Cases Needed**
121 Larks St.	8' × 9'	72 sq. ft.	slate/$1.19	7
79A Bellingham Dr.	13' × 11'	sq. ft.	quarry tile/$1.77	
9205 Main	27' × 19'	sq. ft.	ceramic/$1.58	
33 Pine Rd.	18' × 16'	sq. ft.	vinyl/$.59	

READ IT •

Look at the labels on paint cans, carpet cleaners, stains, or varnishes. Find where each label
tells how many square feet can be covered or cleaned by the contents of the can. Make a list
of each can's amount and the area the contents will cover. Which products cover a larger area?

Estimating and Problem Solving

In the video program, you saw some examples of how and when people estimate. As you learned, estimating is simply using numbers that are close but not exact. People may estimate because some numbers are easier to work with than others and because they do not always need an exact answer.

One common way to estimate is called **front-end estimation,** and it is used when the numbers you are working with are large. Suppose you want a quick estimate of the difference between $3365.83 and $5231.15. To use front-end estimation, subtract the **lead digits** (the first digit in a number). In this case, the lead digits are both in the thousands place, so you subtract 3 from 5.

$$\begin{array}{r} \$5231.15 \\ -\ \ 3365.83 \\ \hline \end{array} \qquad \begin{array}{r} 5 \\ -\ 3 \\ \hline 2 \end{array}$$ *The answer is about $2000.*

To get a closer estimate, try using the *two* lead digits in each number.

$$\begin{array}{r} \$5231.15 \\ -\ \ 3365.83 \\ \hline \end{array} \qquad \begin{array}{r} 52 \\ -\ 33 \\ \hline 19 \end{array}$$ *The answer is about $1900.*

When using front-end estimation, you still have to line up digits with the same place value.

Use front-end estimation to estimate the answer to each problem. Use the first two digits to get a closer estimate. (Remember ≈ means *is approximately equal to*.)

1. 1315 + 2220 ≈ _____
2. 4345 − 1250 ≈ _____
3. 19,560 + 22,500 ≈ _____
4. 6789 − 3501 ≈ _____

5. 95,600 − 23,150 ≈ _____
6. 4136 + 8500 ≈ _____
7. 2950 − 1120 ≈ _____
8. 20,900 + 10,550 ≈ _____

Compatible Pairs

To make estimating with division much easier, you can use **compatible pairs** of numbers. Compatible numbers are numbers that divide exactly. To use the compatible pair method when estimating, find numbers that are close to the original numbers but are easy to divide.

$6\overline{)349}$ does not divide evenly, but $6\overline{)360}$ does.
So $6\overline{)349}$ is approximately **60.**

$9\overline{)211}$ does not divide evenly, but $9\overline{)180}$ does.
So $9\overline{)211}$ is approximately **20.**

Use compatible pairs to estimate answers to these problems.

1. $532 \div 5 \approx$ _____
2. $233 \div 6 \approx$ _____
3. $773 \div 9 \approx$ _____
4. $617 \div 3 \approx$ _____

Estimation and the Calculator

As you've seen in the video program, calculators are handy tools on the job. A calculator is quick and easy to use. And if you enter numbers and operations correctly, calculators almost never make mistakes.

But even work on a calculator should be checked. For example, if a person makes a mistake and inputs 100 instead of 1000, imagine how wrong the calculator answer will be! A good check to be sure the calculator is displaying a reasonable answer is to estimate the answer.

Suppose you want to add 3554 and 2419 on a calculator. You enter what you think are the correct numbers and see this result on the display:

$$2975.$$

Now use front-end estimation to add the two numbers:

$$
\begin{array}{rcl}
3554 & \approx & 3500 \\
2419 & \approx & 2400 \\
\hline
 & & 5900
\end{array}
$$

Your estimate is 5900. If you compare this estimate to the calculator display, you'll realize that you must have made a mistake entering the numbers. If you do the calculation again, you'll find the actual answer is **5973.** This answer is much closer to your estimate.

Use estimation to check the calculator displays below. If the display is incorrect, write the correct amount on the line provided.

1. $6797 \div 7 =$ $971.$ _____
2. $786 - 328 =$ $1214.$ _____
3. $22{,}934 \times 4 =$ $22938.$ _____
4. $1409 + 3167 =$ $5526.$ _____
5. $5520 \times 2 =$ $10000.$ _____
6. $490 \div 2 =$ $245.$ _____
7. $3198 - 1086 =$ $1100.$ _____
8. $5602 + 4449 =$ $10051.$ _____

RETAIL: Nina Polovchek is a salesperson at Bloom's Sporting Goods. Her job involves working with customers, merchandise, and money. As with most jobs that include handling money, Nina's job requires her to be careful and accurate. She knows she needs to check any math calculations.

At the end of each day, stores often require employees to fill out a **reconciliation sheet,** which is sometimes also called a balance sheet. On this sheet a salesperson records the amount of money in the cash drawer at the beginning of the day. He or she then writes down information about what money came in during the day and what money went out. This final amount should match the amount recorded by the cash register.

Problem Solving

One of Nina's jobs is to quickly check that the balance recorded on the reconciliation sheet is accurate. This is a time when her estimation skills are useful.

Nina used the information below to fill out the reconciliation sheet on the next page. To determine whether the final balance makes sense, follow the steps on the next page.

Beginning Drawer Balance: $485.50

Sales		Coupons Redeemed	
9 A.M.–12 P.M.	$290.77	9 A.M.–12 P.M.	$8.00
12 P.M.–3 P.M.	$401.55	12 P.M.–3 P.M.	$0.00
3 P.M.–6 P.M.	$288.32	3 P.M.–6 P.M.	$20.00

Refunds		Gift Certificates Redeemed	
9 A.M.–12 P.M.	$0.00	9 A.M.–12 P.M.	$0.00
12 P.M.–3 P.M.	$5.99	12 P.M.–3 P.M.	$100.00
3 P.M.–6 P.M.	$42.98	3 P.M.–6 P.M.	$0.00

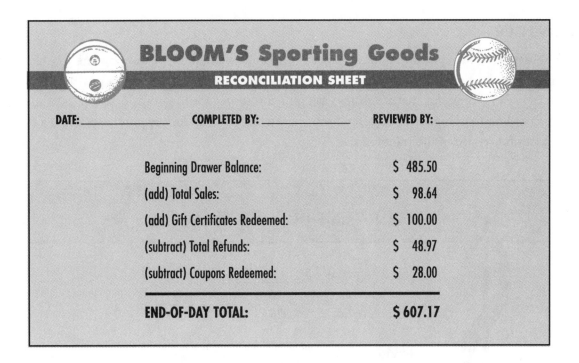

BLOOM'S Sporting Goods

RECONCILIATION SHEET

DATE: _____   COMPLETED BY: _____   REVIEWED BY: _____

Beginning Drawer Balance:	$ 485.50
(add) Total Sales:	$ 98.64
(add) Gift Certificates Redeemed:	$ 100.00
(subtract) Total Refunds:	$ 48.97
(subtract) Coupons Redeemed:	$ 28.00
END-OF-DAY TOTAL:	**$ 607.17**

1. Use front-end estimation to check each of the amounts recorded on the reconciliation sheet above. If your estimate is close to the figure given, put a check mark next to it.

2. If your estimate is not close to the amount given, use a calculator to check the addition or subtraction. Cross out the incorrect amount, and write in the correct one.

3. Use your calculator to find the corrected end-of-day total. Read carefully so that the appropriate amounts are added or subtracted.

COMMUNICATE ●

Suppose you found a mistake in the calculations of a co-worker. What do you think you would do? How would you like the situation to be handled if it were you who had made the mistake?

Use the space below to tell how you would handle the situation and why.

_____

_____

_____

_____

_____

_____

Review

When Doug Silverstein ran out of paper in the middle of an important copying job, his boss at the real estate office gave him money from petty cash to buy some at a nearby store. Petty cash refers to money that a business has on hand to pay for the occasional needs of the office. According to company policy, Doug returned with a receipt for his purchase, and his boss kept a careful record of the transaction.

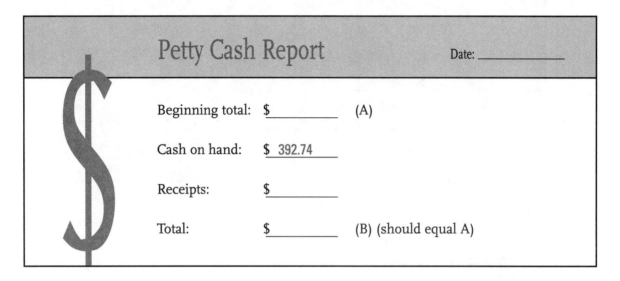

Petty Cash Report   Date: _____

Beginning total: $_____ (A)

Cash on hand: $ 392.74

Receipts: $_____

Total: $_____ (B) (should equal A)

A petty cash report is shown above, with some of the information already filled in. "Cash on hand" refers to the amount of money actually in the petty cash drawer or envelope at this time. Below you'll find several receipts from purchases made with the petty cash. Following the receipts is a table listing information about the money in petty cash at the start of the day. Use all of this information to answer the questions that follow. You may use a calculator for all or part of the exercise.

deluxe bakery

12	choc. cupcakes	4.80
1½	dozen sugar cookies	5.20
2	doz. bagels	18.75
3	lemon pies	22.65

TOTAL: $51.40

BEST Office Supplies

2 boxes #2 pencils @ $3.99 ea		$7.98
12 file folders @ $.29 ea		$3.48
2 3-ring binders @ $2.99 ea		$5.98
2 boxes thumbtacks @ $1.39 ea		$2.78
	SUBTOTAL	$20.22
	TAX 5%	1.01
	TOTAL	$21.23

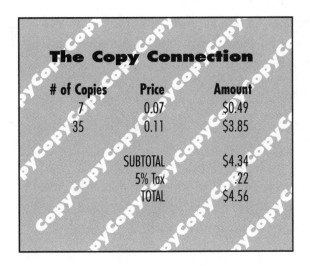

The Copy Connection

# of Copies	Price	Amount
7	0.07	$0.49
35	0.11	$3.85
	SUBTOTAL	$4.34
	5% Tax	.22
	TOTAL	$4.56

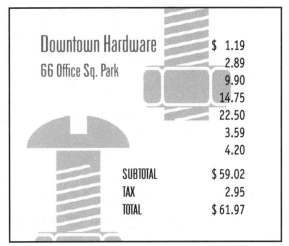

Downtown Hardware
66 Office Sq. Park

	$ 1.19
	2.89
	9.90
	14.75
	22.50
	3.59
	4.20
SUBTOTAL	$ 59.02
TAX	2.95
TOTAL	$ 61.97

casual catering

chicken salad platter. $3.95
Greek salad...................................4.95
vegetable soup 2.50

diet cola $0.95
coffee 0.80
skim milk 1.00

TOTAL $14.15

DISCOUNT
FURNITURE WAREHOUSE

one polished steel bookcase
3 ft. by 5 ft. by 1 ft.

$48.95

Petty Cash Drawer
(start of day 4/12)

$100 bills:	2
$ 50 bills:	2
$ 20 bills:	6
$ 10 bills:	10
$ 5 bills:	10
$ 1 bills:	25

1. How much money was in the petty cash drawer at the start of the business day on 4/12?
   Write this total on line (A) of the petty cash report.

2. What was the total amount in petty cash receipts, including purchases made at Deluxe Bakery, Best Office Supplies, The Copy Connection, Downtown Hardware, Casual Catering, and Discount Furniture Warehouse? Write this amount in the space labeled "Receipts" on the petty cash report.

3. Add the total receipts to the cash on hand. Write this amount on line (B). Does this total match line (A)?

4. The employee who took out petty cash to purchase baked goods remembered that she had bought one lemon pie for her own family. She gave money back to petty cash to cover the expense herself. How much did she give back to petty cash? _____

5. Fill out a new petty cash report reflecting the change described above in problem 4.

Petty Cash Report   Date: _____

Beginning total: $_____ (A)

Cash on hand: $_____

Receipts: $_____

Total: $_____ (B) (should equal A)

Fractions, Decimals, and Percents

OBJECTIVES

In this lesson, you will work with these math concepts and skills to do workplace tasks:

1. Understanding and using decimals
2. Understanding and using fractions
3. Understanding and using ratios, proportions, and percents

Workplace math often involves numbers less than one—decimal places to show cents on a dollar and socket set sizes listed as fractions of an inch. Workplace math also measures parts of a whole—the fraction of total output that is defective and the percent raise workers will get. To express numbers less than one and parts of a whole, we use fractions, decimals, and percents.

The video program you are about to watch will show how fractions, decimals, and percents are used in the workplace. As you watch the program, pay attention to how people express these numbers. When do they use fractions? decimals? percents? For example, measuring usually includes fractions or decimals, but statistics often uses percents.

Using fractions, decimals, and percents is more common than we often realize. As you watch the video, think about how often you use numbers to express parts of a whole every day.

Sneak Preview

This exercise previews some of the concepts from Program 22. After you answer the questions, use the Feedback on page 55 to help set your learning goals.

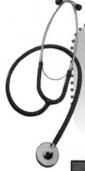

HEALTH CARE: Frank Lavitad works as a safety and sanitation aide at a large nursing home. As with any job in a health care environment, his work requires attention to details. He must fill out a form like the one below so that his supervisor can track his team's progress.

Team Member Shift Report		room cleaned	total hours
		404A	0.5
Name: Frank Lavitad		404B	0.5
Shift: A		406	1.25
		408A	1.25
Date: 7/16		408B	1.5
Current hourly wage: $ 5.40		410	1.5

Please check off supply quantities used today. Estimate when necessary.				
rubber gloves	1 pair	✓2 pairs	3 pairs	other _____
antiseptic hand soap	1 cup	✓$1\frac{1}{2}$ cups	2 cups	$2\frac{1}{2}$ cups
T-bowl cleaner	$1\frac{1}{2}$ pints	$2\frac{1}{2}$ pints	✓$4\frac{1}{2}$ pints	6 pints
ammonia	1 gallon	$1\frac{1}{2}$ gallons	2 gallons	✓$2\frac{1}{2}$ gallons
window cleaner	$\frac{1}{4}$ bottle	$\frac{1}{2}$ bottle	✓$\frac{3}{4}$ bottle	1 bottle

Answer these questions based on the report.

1. What total number of hours did Frank work on this day?

   (1) 8
   (2) 7
   (3) 6.5
   (4) 6
   (5) 5.25

2. Based on the hourly wage listed, how much did Frank earn cleaning room 408A?

   (1) $1.25
   (2) $4.50
   (3) $6.75
   (4) $67.50
   (5) $90.25

3. Approximately how much toilet bowl (T-bowl) cleaner did Frank use in each of the six rooms he cleaned?

(1) $4\frac{1}{2}$ pints   (4) $1\frac{1}{2}$ pints

(2) $10\frac{1}{2}$ pints   (5) $\frac{3}{4}$ pint

(3) 2 pints

4. The jug of ammonia Frank used originally held 5 gallons. How many gallons were left at the end of this day?

(1) 2   (4) $4\frac{1}{2}$

(2) $2\frac{1}{2}$ (5) $7\frac{1}{2}$

(3) $3\frac{1}{2}$

5. There are 25 rooms on the 5th floor of the nursing home. Frank's team cleaned 20 of them. What percent of the 5th floor rooms did his team clean?

(1) 20   (4) 50

(2) 25   (5) 80

(3) 45

Feedback

- If you got all of the questions right . . .   you have a foundation for working with decimals, fractions, and percents. Concentrate on how these kinds of numbers are used in the video program.

- If you missed question 1 . . .   you need to work on adding decimals.

- If you missed question 2 . . .   you need to learn more about multiplying decimals.

- If you missed question 3 . . .   concentrate on learning how to divide fractions.

- If you missed question 4 . . .   pay special attention to subtracting fractions.

- If you missed question 5 . . .   you need to work on your percent skills.

Answers for Sneak Preview:

1. Choice (3)   2. Choice (3)   3. Choice (5)   4. Choice (2)   5. Choice (5)

Vocabulary for *Fractions, Decimals, and Percents*

common denominators   the denominators that are the same in two or more fractions

consumed   eaten or drunk up; used up

cross products   results of multiplying the numerator of each fraction in a proportion by the denominator of the other

denominator   the bottom number in a fraction; tells how many parts the whole is divided into

improper fraction   a fraction with a numerator equal to or greater than its denominator

mixed number   a number made up of a whole number and a fraction

numerator   the top number in a fraction; tells how many parts of the whole there are

proportion   an expression that says two fractions (ratios) are equal

reciprocal   a fraction with numerator and denominator reversed

specifications   details or descriptions that tell how something is to be constructed or made

standards   levels of excellence against which something or someone is judged or compared

tolerance   the amount by which a measure is allowed to vary

variable   a letter of the alphabet (such as *a*, *b*, or *x*) that stands for an unknown number

PBS LiteracyLink®

Now watch Program 22.

After you watch, work on:
- pages 57–72 in this workbook
- Internet activities at www.pbs.org/literacy

AFTER you WATCH

Fractions, Decimals, and Percents

WORKTIP

Whenever you do calculations on the job:

- Be sure to write numbers neatly and correctly.
- Know ahead of time whether you want your answer to be a whole number, fraction, decimal, or percent.
- Use a calculator when possible, but remember that your answer will be in decimal form.
- Use number sense to get an idea of the size of the answer you're expecting.

On the following pages, you will learn more about the math skills discussed in the video program: decimals, fractions, and percents. You'll also have the opportunity to practice these skills and others.

Think About the Key Points from the Video Program

- Fractions, decimals, and percents all represent parts of a whole. The whole could be a day, an hour, or an amount of money.
- Different forms are used for different applications. For example, percents are commonly used to show discounts, while fractions are common in measurements. The ability to convert one form to another is a helpful job skill.
- There are many ways to approach and solve a problem. Find a way that makes sense to you. Use your number sense to estimate or check your calculations.

Reading Decimals

Just as whole numbers have place values, so do decimals. In fact, you are already familiar with two decimal place values—tenths and hundredths—from using our money system. The number of decimal place values is unlimited, but most of your work on the job will require you to use decimals only as far as the thousandths place.

two hundred fifty   nine thousandths

250.009

The decimal point is read as "and."

When you read a decimal number, say the number and place value of the last digit. The number above is read as "two hundred fifty and nine thousandths." How would you read the decimal 3.08?

You are right if you said "three and eight hundredths." Notice that the zero holds the 8 in the hundredths place. For more information on reading decimals, turn to page 147 of the Reference Handbook.

Read each value below, then write it in number form. The first one has been done for you.

1. ten and fourteen hundredths _10.14_

2. twenty-one and fourteen thousandths _____

3. one hundred five and six tenths _____

4. sixty-two and ten thousandths _____

Comparing Decimals

When you compare decimals, first be sure that each has the same number of digits. If they do not, add zeros at the end of the shorter decimal until they do. For example, which is larger, 3.25 or 3.5?

3.25

3.50   *You can add a zero after the last digit without changing its value; 3.5 = 3.50.*

Now compare just as you would with whole numbers. 3.5 is larger than 3.25 because 50 is larger than 25.

Circle the larger decimal.

1. 10.09 or 10.9   3. 5.702   or   5.72

2. 4.005 or 4.511   4. 85.056 or 85.06

Adding and Subtracting Decimals

When you add or subtract decimals, be sure to line up decimal point under decimal point, just as you learned when you worked with money. Add zeros to help you keep track of place value if you wish. What is 14.97 added to 2.6?

$$
\begin{array}{r}
14.97 \\
+\ \ 2.60 \\
\hline
17.57
\end{array}
$$

Add this zero to help you keep digits lined up.

Add or subtract as indicated.

1. $15.5 + 10.75 =$ _____
2. $5.048 - 1.7 =$ _____
3. $11.625 + 9.9 =$ _____
4. $25.8 - 12.095 =$ _____
5. $48.9 + 4.04 =$ _____
6. $9.74 - 3.4 =$ _____

Multiplying and Dividing Decimals

When you multiply decimals, work just as you would with whole numbers. Then decide where to put the decimal point by adding up the number of digits following the decimal points in the two numbers you are multiplying.

$$
\begin{array}{r}
9.55 \\
\times\ \ \ .3 \\
\hline
\mathbf{2.865}
\end{array}
$$

2 digits after decimal point
1 digit after decimal point
3 digits after decimal point

When you divide decimals, be sure to bring the decimal point up directly above the decimal point in the dividend.

Bring the decimal point directly up.

$$
\begin{array}{r}
1.9 \\
5\overline{)9.5} \\
\underline{5} \\
4\,5 \\
\underline{4\,5} \\
0
\end{array}
$$

For more information on dividing decimals, turn to page 148 in the Reference Handbook.

Multiply or divide as indicated.

1. $4.66 \times 3.1 =$ _____
2. $10.8 \div 25 =$ _____
3. $15.09 \times 21.5 =$ _____
4. $106.85 \div 5 =$ _____
5. $14.7 \times 3.1 =$ _____
6. $2.24 \div 4 =$ _____

WorkSkills

MANUFACTURING: Sherry Johnson is a quality-control technician on an assembly line that makes plastic parts for automobiles. Her job involves making sure that the parts are up to company **standards.** No product can ever be perfect, but Sherry's company must be sure that its products are as good as possible.

On the next page you will find a quality-control inspection sheet for Sherry's assembly line. Hundreds of parts come off the line every hour. Sherry removes a sample from the line every half hour and takes five measurements. For the part to be up to company standards, each measurement must be within a certain range, or **tolerance.**

Problem Solving

Look under the column labeled "Tolerance." Find the tolerance for Side A: 1.5 millimeters $\pm$.25 millimeters. A tolerance of $\pm$.25 (plus or minus .25 millimeters) means that while the desired measurement is 1.5 mm, any measurement that is .25 mm less or .25 mm more than 1.5 mm is acceptable.

What is the range of acceptable measurements?

$$1.5 - .25 = 1.25 \text{ mm}$$
$$1.5 + .25 = 1.75 \text{ mm}$$

Therefore, a measurement must be between 1.25 mm and 1.75 mm.

Read the quality-control inspection sheet on page 61. It is partly completed. Follow the directions to complete it, then answer the questions on page 61.

1. Write the following measurements in the column labeled 10:30. A co-worker has measured each area and is calling out each measurement to you so that you can record it on the inspection sheet. The first one is done for you.

   a. "Side A is one and seventy-five hundredths millimeters."
   b. "Side B is two and five thousandths millimeters."
   c. "Hole C is one and seven hundredths millimeters."
   d. "Side D is three and fourteen thousandths millimeters."
   e. "Hole E is two and one hundred twenty-nine thousandths millimeters."

Quality-Control Inspection Sheet

Date: January 22
Part # 31-D5PPA

Side/ Hole	Tolerance	Measurements 8:00	8:30	9:00	9:30	10:00	10:30
A	1.5 mm ± .25	1.8	1.73	1.55	1.51	1.69	<u>1.75</u>
B	2.0 mm ± .5	2.019	2.195	1.599	1.75	1.975	_____
C	.9 mm ± .2	0.95	1.1	1.05	1.25	1.3	_____
D	3.0 mm ± .1	3.015	2.95	2.99	3.125	3.005	_____
E	2.3 mm ± .5	1.8	2.15	2.38	1.925	2.12	_____

Answer the questions using the information in the inspection sheet. You may use a calculator.

2. At what time was the Side B measurement the smallest? _____
   At what time was it the largest? _____

3. What is the difference between the measurements of Hole C at 8:00 and 10:00?
   _____

4. What is the range of acceptable measurements for Hole E?
   smallest: _____   largest: _____

5. Company policy requires the assembly line operator to shut down the line when the tolerances are above or below acceptable limits. At what times was the line shut down for:

   a. Side A? _____
   b. Side D? _____

WRITE IT

Our money system is based on the decimal system. **Write a paragraph explaining that idea. Use examples about dollars and cents.**

Understanding and Comparing Fractions

A fraction is another way to express part of a whole. In a fraction, the bottom number, or **denominator,** tells how many parts the whole is divided into. The top number, or **numerator,** tells how many of those parts there are. Look at the figure below. The fraction $\frac{3}{5}$ tells you that the whole is divided into 5 parts and 3 of those parts are shaded.

$\frac{3}{5}$ ←——— numerator (number of parts shaded)
←——— denominator (total number of parts)

To compare fractions, you must make sure that the fractions have the same denominator. Which is greater, $\frac{8}{9}$ or $\frac{5}{9}$? Because 8 parts out of 9 is greater than 5 parts out of 9, you know that $\frac{8}{9}$ is greater than $\frac{5}{9}$.

Which is greater, $\frac{3}{4}$ or $\frac{5}{8}$? In this case, you can change $\frac{3}{4}$ so that it has a denominator of 8.

$\frac{3}{4} = \frac{?}{8}$

$\frac{3}{4} \times \frac{2}{2} = \frac{6}{8}$ *When converting a fraction, you must multiply the numerator and denominator by the same amount.*

Now you can compare $\frac{6}{8}$ and $\frac{5}{8}$. Since $\frac{6}{8} > \frac{5}{8}$, you know that $\frac{3}{4} > \frac{5}{8}$. (If you need help with **common denominators,** turn to page 149 in the Reference Handbook.)

Circle the larger fraction in each pair. Find common denominators when necessary.

1. $\frac{2}{3}$ or $\frac{5}{6}$ 3. $\frac{2}{9}$ or $\frac{7}{9}$ 5. $\frac{13}{20}$ or $\frac{3}{4}$

2. $\frac{1}{4}$ or $\frac{1}{5}$ 4. $\frac{3}{4}$ or $\frac{2}{3}$ 6. $\frac{5}{6}$ or $\frac{11}{12}$

Adding and Subtracting Fractions

Fractions must have the same denominator in order to be added or subtracted. Once they have the same denominator, add or subtract the numerators, and use the common denominator in the answer.

EXAMPLE 1

$\frac{2}{3} = \frac{6}{9}$
$+\frac{1}{9} = \frac{1}{9}$
$\frac{7}{9}$

EXAMPLE 2

$\frac{2}{5} = \frac{4}{10}$
$-\frac{1}{10} = \frac{1}{10}$
$\frac{3}{10}$

Sometimes when you add or subtract fractions, you may need to change an **improper fraction** (such as $\frac{9}{5}$) to a **mixed number** ($1\frac{4}{5}$). Or you may have to simplify a fraction to lowest terms ($\frac{6}{9} = \frac{2}{3}$). For help with these skills, turn to page 149 in the Reference Handbook.

Add or subtract these fractions as indicated. Be sure to find a common denominator if you need to. The first problem has been started for you.

1. $\frac{3}{8} + \frac{1}{4} = \frac{3}{8} + \frac{2}{8} =$ _____   3. $\frac{2}{5} + \frac{2}{5} =$ _____   5. $\frac{7}{12} + \frac{5}{6} =$ _____

2. $\frac{8}{9} - \frac{4}{9} =$ _____   4. $\frac{3}{4} - \frac{1}{8} =$ _____   6. $\frac{8}{10} - \frac{1}{5} =$ _____

Multiplying and Dividing Fractions

Multiplying fractions is a simple process. First multiply the numerators together to find the new numerator. Then multiply the denominators together to find the new denominator.

$$\frac{1}{2} \times \frac{3}{4} = \frac{1 \times 3}{2 \times 4} = \frac{3}{8}$$

To multiply a whole number by a fraction, remember that any number over 1 (divided by 1) is equal to that number. For example, $3 = \frac{3}{1}$ and $15 = \frac{15}{1}$. So to multiply by a whole number, change the whole number to a fraction, then multiply.

$$\frac{3}{4} \times 8 = \frac{3}{4} \times \frac{8}{1} = \frac{24}{4} \quad \text{Simplify } \frac{24}{4}.$$

$$\frac{24}{4} = \frac{24 \div 4}{4 \div 4} = 6$$

To divide by a fraction, you *multiply* by its **reciprocal.** A reciprocal is the fraction with its numerator and denominator reversed. For example, the reciprocal of $\frac{3}{5}$ is $\frac{5}{3}$, and the reciprocal of $\frac{1}{8}$ is $\frac{8}{1}$. To divide $\frac{2}{3}$ by $\frac{1}{2}$, multiply $\frac{2}{3}$ by the reciprocal of $\frac{1}{2}$, which is $\frac{2}{1}$.

$$\frac{2}{3} \div \frac{1}{2} = \frac{2}{3} \times \frac{2}{1} = \frac{4}{3}$$

Write $\frac{4}{3}$ as a proper fraction. $\frac{4}{3}$ means $4 \div 3$, which equals 1 remainder 1.

$$\frac{4}{3} = 1\frac{1}{3} \longleftarrow \textit{remainder}$$

Multiply or divide these fractions.

1. $\frac{1}{3} \times \frac{2}{5} =$ _____   3. $\frac{1}{6} \div \frac{1}{3} =$ _____   5. $\frac{2}{3} \times \frac{4}{5} =$ _____

2. $\frac{9}{10} \times 100 =$ _____   4. $\frac{1}{2} \div \frac{1}{4} =$ _____   6. $\frac{1}{3} \div \frac{9}{10} =$ _____

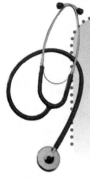

HEALTH CARE: Many jobs in health care require work with menus and food. After all, many aspects of our health are directly related to what we eat. Monica, a dietary aide, works with doctors and nurses to ensure that patients are fed a balanced diet that will help them get well. Monica pays attention to such things as calories, vitamins, minerals, and fat content.

Below you'll find a dietary aide log in which Monica recorded the foods offered to one patient over the course of one day. At the beginning of the day, Monica wrote out what the doctor and dietitian agreed is a sensible menu for the patient. At the end of the day, she also estimates how much of each meal the patient actually **consumed** (ate).

Dietary Aide Log			Patient: Ambrose Conroy Date: 6/19	
BREAKFAST	**Amount Served**	**Total Calories**	**Sodium (mg)**	**Amount Consumed**
scrambled egg	1	110	155	$\frac{1}{2}$
bacon	1 slice	45	101	all
oatmeal	$\frac{3}{4}$ cup	65	105	$\frac{1}{2}$
orange juice	$5\frac{1}{2}$ oz.	90	2	$\frac{3}{4}$
milk, skim	8 oz.	90	126	all
LUNCH				
roasted chicken	$3\frac{1}{2}$ oz.	180	72	$\frac{1}{3}$
stewed tomatoes	$\frac{1}{2}$ cup	65	280	$\frac{1}{2}$
wild rice	$\frac{2}{3}$ cup	105	400	$\frac{1}{2}$
tea	1 cup	0	3	all
DINNER				
broiled trout	$3\frac{1}{2}$ oz.	240	82	$\frac{1}{2}$
hash brown potatoes	$1\frac{1}{2}$ cups	325	300	$\frac{1}{4}$
coleslaw	$\frac{3}{4}$ cup	175	25	$\frac{1}{2}$
brownie	1 small	150	45	all
milk, skim	8 oz.	90	126	$\frac{1}{2}$

Problem Solving

Using Monica's estimate of what fraction of each food the patient ate, you can figure out how many calories and how much sodium the patient consumed.

For example, the log indicates that the patient ate $\frac{1}{3}$ of the $3\frac{1}{2}$ ounces of chicken at lunch. How many ounces of chicken were actually consumed? Multiply to find out. "One-third of" means "one-third times."

ounces of chicken served

$$\frac{1}{3} \times 3\frac{1}{2} = ?$$

portion patient ate

Before you can multiply a mixed number, you have to change it to an improper fraction. Multiply the whole number by the denominator, then add the numerator. Put the total over the original denominator.

$$3\frac{1}{2} = \frac{(3 \times 2) + 1}{2} = \frac{7}{2}$$ ⟵ *To change $3\frac{1}{2}$ to an improper fraction, multiply the whole number (3) by the denominator (2). Then add the numerator (1).*

$$\frac{1}{3} \times \frac{7}{2} = \frac{7}{6}$$ ounces of chicken ⟵ *Multiply to find the amount.*

How would you write $\frac{7}{6}$ ounces of chicken? Remember that $\frac{7}{6}$ means $7 \div 6 = 1$ r1.

$$\frac{7}{6} = 1\frac{1}{6} \text{ oz.}$$

Use Monica's dietary aide log to answer these questions.

1. How many calories were in the orange juice that was consumed? (Hint: $\frac{3}{4}$ of 90 calories)

   _____

2. What fraction of a cup of oatmeal did the patient eat? (Hint: $\frac{1}{2}$ of $\frac{3}{4}$ cup of oatmeal)

   _____

3. How many milligrams of sodium were in the roasted chicken the patient consumed?

   _____

4. What fraction of a cup of stewed tomatoes did the patient eat?_____

5. How many milligrams of sodium were in the wild rice consumed by the patient?_____

TECH TIP ·

Most calculators show decimals but not fractions. To work with fractions using a calculator, change them to decimals. To do this, divide the numerator by the denominator. For example, to change $\frac{3}{4}$ to a decimal, enter the numerator (3), then the division sign, then the denominator (4), then the equal sign: $3 \div 4 = 0.75$.

What is $\frac{7}{8}$ written as a decimal? $\frac{3}{5}$? Use a calculator to find out.

Understanding Proportion and Percent

A **proportion** is a set of two equal fractions. (To review equivalent, or equal, fractions, turn to page 148 in the Reference Handbook.) Proportions can be used to solve all kinds of problems.

If a term (number) in a proportion is unknown, you can find its value because the cross products are equal. A **cross product** is the result of multiplying the numerator of one fraction by the denominator of the other fraction in a proportion. How can we find the value of **variable** a in the proportion below? Use cross products.

$$\frac{9}{15} = \frac{a}{5}$$ ⟵ *Multiply 9 and 5 to find one cross product.*
Multiply 15 and a to find the other cross product.

$$9 \times 5 = 15 \times a$$
$$45 = 15 \times a$$ ⟵ *What do you multiply 15 by to get 45?*
$$45 \div 15 = a$$
$$3 = a$$ ⟵ *Check: 15 × 3 = 45*

For help in solving equations, turn to page 152 in the Reference Handbook.

Find the missing term in each proportion below.

1. $\frac{2}{7} = \frac{4}{a}$

2. $\frac{3}{4} = \frac{b}{100}$

3. $\frac{x}{10} = \frac{14}{5}$

4. $\frac{1}{y} = \frac{9}{27}$

5. $\frac{x}{3} = \frac{14}{6}$

6. $\frac{2}{9} = \frac{6}{a}$

Writing Percents

A percent is just another way to express a part of a whole. In this case, the whole is always divided into 100 equal parts. Percent means "out of 100." What percent of the square below is shaded?

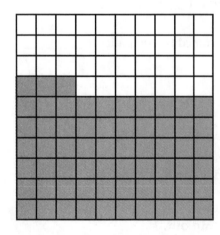

Since 63 parts are shaded, we can say that 63% of the square is shaded. We can also say that $\frac{63}{100}$ or .63 is shaded.

$$63\% = \frac{63}{100} = .63$$

Knowing how to change decimals and fractions to percents and vice versa is a very important skill in the workplace. Turn to page 150 in the Reference Handbook for help with this skill.

Write the part of each figure that is shaded. Express the part as a percent, a fraction, and a decimal.

1. percent ____ fraction ____ decimal ____

3. percent ____ fraction ____ decimal ____

2. percent ____ fraction ____ decimal ____

4. percent ____ fraction ____ decimal ____

Solving Percent Problems

Understanding proportions will help you solve all kinds of percent problems. Remember that in any percent problem, the proportion compares the part to the whole.

$$\frac{PART}{WHOLE} = \frac{PART}{WHOLE}$$

And, as you learned earlier, percent is always expressed as a part of 100. Therefore, 100 is always a denominator in one of the fractions.

What is 30% of 150? You must find the part. Set up a proportion.

$$percent \longrightarrow \frac{30}{100} = \frac{a}{150} \longleftarrow \begin{array}{l} part \\ whole \end{array}$$

Use cross products to find the missing term.

$$30 \times 150 = 100 \times a$$
$$4500 = 100 \times a$$
$$4500 \div 100 = a$$
$$\mathbf{45 = a} \longleftarrow \textit{45 is 30\% of 150.}$$

Use proportions to solve these percent problems.

1. 45 is what percent of 180?

$$\frac{x}{100} = \frac{45}{180}$$

3. What is 15% of 500?

$$\frac{15}{100} = \frac{y}{500}$$

2. 75 is 10% of what number?

$$\frac{10}{100} = \frac{75}{a}$$

4. 40% of 220 is what?

$$\frac{40}{100} = \frac{x}{220}$$

WorkSkills

MANUFACTURING: Philip Ngomo is a production assistant for a large bagel manufacturer, a job that involves many different tasks. Philip records how many items are produced over a period of time and how many were shipped out. He also records information about products thrown away because they were defective. In all of these cases, he needs accurate control of numbers.

Below you'll find a production and throwaway sheet used by Philip's company. Philip has recorded how many bagels were made and how many were thrown away each day for one week.

Problem Solving

Follow the steps on page 69 to complete the production sheet below.

Weekly Bagel Production and Throwaway Sheet
WEEK OF: _October 20_

Flavor	Monday	Tuesday	Wednesday	Thursday	Friday	TOTAL
plain	_220_ baked _11_ thrown away	_300_ baked _20_ thrown away	_300_ baked _10_ thrown away	_220_ baked _22_ thrown away	_560_ baked _28_ thrown away	_1600_ baked _91_ thrown away
onion	_150_ baked _30_ thrown away	_120_ baked _10_ thrown away	_200_ baked _25_ thrown away	_220_ baked _11_ thrown away	_400_ baked _20_ thrown away	___ baked ___ thrown away
sesame	_140_ baked _7_ thrown away	_240_ baked _8_ thrown away	_250_ baked _25_ thrown away	_100_ baked _4_ thrown away	_200_ baked _12_ thrown away	___ baked ___ thrown away
salt	_170_ baked _34_ thrown away	_200_ baked _6_ thrown away	_220_ baked _22_ thrown away	_180_ baked _10_ thrown away	_340_ baked _17_ thrown away	___ baked ___ thrown away
garlic	_220_ baked _11_ thrown away	_220_ baked _11_ thrown away	_220_ baked _11_ thrown away	_220_ baked _11_ thrown away	_220_ baked _11_ thrown away	___ baked ___ thrown away
cinnamon raisin	_500_ baked _25_ thrown away	_200_ baked _10_ thrown away	_300_ baked _15_ thrown away	_220_ baked _11_ thrown away	_620_ baked _31_ thrown away	___ baked ___ thrown away
TOTAL	_1400_ baked _118_ thrown away	___ baked ___ thrown away	___ baked ___ thrown away	___ baked ___ thrown away	___ baked ___ thrown away	___ baked ___ thrown away

1. On the page 68, fill in the Total column *for each day* by adding up the total bagels baked and total thrown away. Monday has been filled in for you.

2. On page 68, fill in the Total row for each flavor bagel by adding up the total bagels baked and the total thrown away. Plain has been filled in for you.

3. Using the numbers found in steps 1 and 2, use a calculator to find the percent throwaway for each day and flavor and for each day's total. Divide the number of bagels thrown away by the number of bagels baked. Use your calculator when you need to. Round to the nearest percent, and record the percentages in the chart below.

Percent Throwaways

Flavor	Monday	Tuesday	Wednesday	Thursday	Friday	TOTAL
plain	%	%	%	%	%	%
onion	%	%	%	%	%	%
sesame	5 %	3 %	%	%	%	%
salt	%	%	%	6 %	%	%
garlic	%	%	%	%	%	5 %
cinnamon raisin	%	%	5 %	%	5 %	%
TOTAL	8 %	%	%	%	%	%

READ IT •

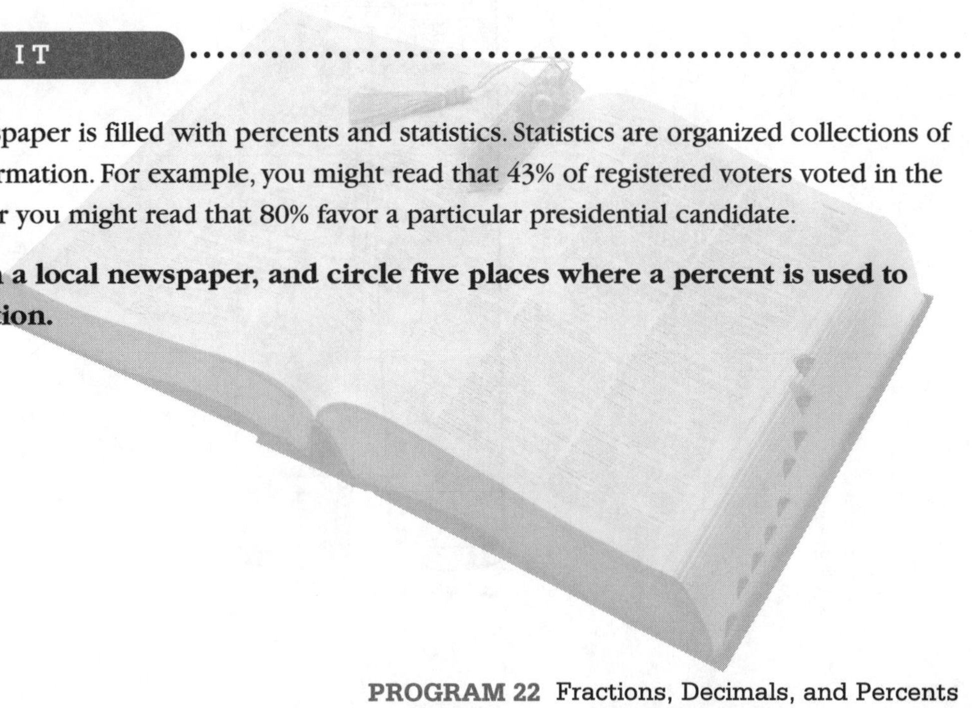

The daily newspaper is filled with percents and statistics. Statistics are organized collections of numerical information. For example, you might read that 43% of registered voters voted in the last election. Or you might read that 80% favor a particular presidential candidate.

Look through a local newspaper, and circle five places where a percent is used to give information.

Review

Workers in the garment or clothing industry spend time measuring, cutting, and sewing fabric. They need to be able to read **specifications** that tell what color, size, and material to use on each order. In this review, you'll have the opportunity to work with specifications for athletic pants in three different sizes. Use your understanding of decimals, fractions, and percents to answer the questions that follow.

Notice that on the drawing of the pants, each dimension (waist, inseam, leg hem, etc.) is labeled with a letter. These letters tell you which dimension is being measured, as identified in the first column of the table below.

Measurements and Tolerances Tough-Go Athletic Pants				
SIDE	**Small**	**Medium**	**Large**	**Tolerance**
A: Back Seam	$10\frac{1}{2}$ inches	12 inches	$14\frac{1}{2}$ inches	$\pm\frac{1}{2}$ inch
B: Inseam	$11\frac{1}{2}$ inches	$14\frac{1}{8}$ inches	$16\frac{1}{2}$ inches	$\pm\frac{1}{2}$ inch
C: Leg Hem	$8\frac{3}{4}$ inches	$9\frac{1}{4}$ inches	$10\frac{1}{2}$ inches	$\pm\frac{3}{4}$ inch
D: Waist	21 inches	$23\frac{1}{4}$ inches	$25\frac{1}{2}$ inches	$\pm\frac{1}{4}$ inch
E: Thigh	$8\frac{1}{2}$ inches	$9\frac{9}{16}$ inches	$10\frac{3}{16}$ inches	$\pm\frac{1}{4}$ inch
Total fabric required	$1\frac{5}{8}$ yards	$2\frac{1}{4}$ yards	$2\frac{7}{8}$ yards	

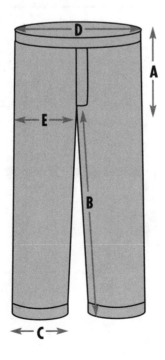

1. How many yards of fabric would be required to make 24 pairs of small athletic pants?

   (1) 14
   (2) 24
   (3) 39

2. There are 40 yards of fabric left in a garment worker's machine. How many pairs of medium athletic pants can be made from this cloth? (Remember that a remainder is not enough for a whole pair of pants.)

   (1) 17
   (2) 18
   (3) 20

3. The fabric used to make a pair of large athletic pants costs $.99 per yard. Estimate the total cost of the fabric for this pair of pants.

   (1) $2.00
   (2) $3.00
   (3) $4.00

For each pair of pants below, decide whether the measurements are within the tolerances allowed. Circle any measurements that are not within the tolerances given in the chart.

4.
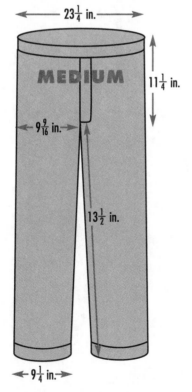

5.
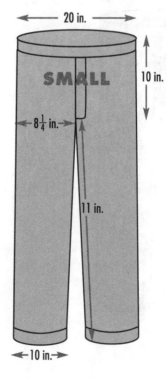

6.

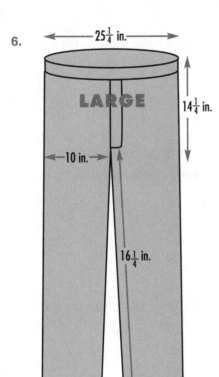

25 $\frac{1}{4}$ in.

14 $\frac{1}{4}$ in.

LARGE

10 in.

16 $\frac{1}{4}$ in.

9 in.

7.

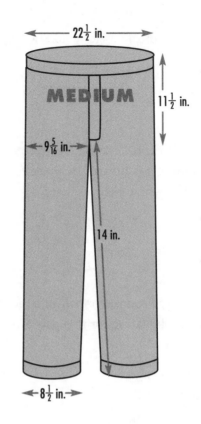

22 $\frac{1}{2}$ in.

11 $\frac{1}{2}$ in.

MEDIUM

9 $\frac{5}{16}$ in.

14 in.

8 $\frac{1}{2}$ in.

8.

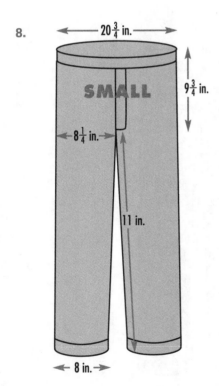

20 $\frac{3}{4}$ in.

9 $\frac{3}{4}$ in.

SMALL

8 $\frac{1}{4}$ in.

11 in.

8 in.

Measurements and Formulas

OBJECTIVES

In this lesson, you will work with these math concepts and skills to do workplace tasks:

1. Measuring using the English system and calculating with English measurements
2. Measuring using the metric system and calculating with metric measurements
3. Choosing formulas and using them to solve problems with measurements

The video program you are about to watch will show how measurement is used in the workplace. You'll see a wide variety of measurement tools, and you'll see how different situations call for different measurement units. You'll also see how workers use **formulas** to gain information about a problem.

As you watch the program, pay attention to how people use measurement to describe something. Watch how different measurement tools are used, and how people record information about length, weight, **diameter,** and so on.

In addition, take some time to think about the things you measure in your life. Remember that time, weight, temperature, and distance are just a few of the measurable parts of our lives.

Sneak Preview

This exercise previews some of the concepts from Program 23. After you answer the questions, use the Feedback on page 75 to help set your learning goals.

RETAIL: Tomas Bravo is employed in the meat and cheese department of a specialty food store. Part of his job involves weighing and pricing different foods. Use the information given on the chart below to help you answer the questions about purchases made in the store where Tomas works.

STANDARD MEASUREMENTS		
1 pound = 16 ounces	8 ounces = 1 cup	1 quart = 2 pints
1000 grams = 1 kilogram	16 ounces = 1 pint	1 gallon = 4 quarts

Circle the correct weight of each product below.

1. (1) $2\frac{1}{2}$ pounds
   (2)   3 pounds
   (3) $3\frac{1}{2}$ pounds

2. (1) $1\frac{3}{4}$ pounds
   (2)   14 ounces
   (3)   1 pound

3. (1)   45 grams
   (2)   400 grams
   (3)   450 grams

4. (1)   1.5 kilograms
   (2)   15 grams
   (3)   15 kilograms

Use the chart to convert the following measurements.

5. 6 cups = _____ ounces

6. 10 quarts = _____ gallons

7. 5.5 kilograms = _____ grams

8. 1500 grams = _____ kilograms

Solve the following problem. Use the chart on page 74 if necessary.

9. A customer buys 250 grams of smoked salmon and 1.75 kilograms of poached salmon. How many kilograms of salmon did he buy in all?

    (1) 251.75   (3) 2

    (2)   2.25   (4) 0.225

Use the formula $C = nr$ (cost = number of units $\times$ rate) to answer this question.

10. A pound of cheddar cheese costs $3.50. How much will $2\frac{1}{2}$ pounds cost?

    (1) $8.75   (3) $1.75

    (2) $5.50   (4) $1.00

Feedback

- If you got all of the questions right . . .   you have a foundation for working with measurements. Concentrate on how different kinds of measurements are used in the video program.

- If you missed question 1 or 2 . . .   you need to work on using English measurement tools.

- If you missed question 3 or 4 . . .   you need to work on using metric measurement tools.

- If you missed question 5 or 6 . . .   concentrate on developing your English measurement conversion skills.

- If you missed question 7 or 8 . . .   pay special attention to your metric conversion skills.

- If you missed question 9 . . .   pay special attention to using the basic operations with measurements.

- If you missed question 10 . . .   focus on using formulas.

10. Choice (1)

Answers for Sneak Preview:
1. Choice (2) 2. Choice (2) 3. Choice (1) 4. Choice (1) 5. 48 6. $2\frac{1}{2}$ 7. 5500 8. 1.5 9. Choice (3)

PROGRAM 23 Measurements and Formulas   75

Vocabulary for *Measurements and Formulas*

caliper an instrument used to measure internal (inside) and external (outer) dimensions

capacity the maximum amount that can be held or contained

conversion factor a number that a measurement is multiplied or divided by in order to convert from one unit to another

convert to change from one unit to another without changing the value of the measurement

diameter the distance across a circle through the center of the circle

formulas equations or statements that show the constant relationship between values

ingredients parts of a recipe or plan that are added to a mixture

micrometer a very precise measurement tool that finds distances as small as a thousandth of an inch

motor skills the ability to use hands, arms, and legs in a productive way

perimeter the distance around a shape

prefix a group of letters added to the beginning of a word to change its meaning

radius half the diameter of a circle; the distance from the center to the edge of a circle

substitute to insert a value in place of a variable

PBS LiteracyLink®

Now watch Program 23.

After you watch, work on:
- pages 77–92 in this workbook
- Internet activities at www.pbs.org/literacy

AFTER•you•WATCH

Measurements and Formulas

On the following pages, you will learn more about the math skills discussed in the video program you have just watched. You'll also have the opportunity to practice these skills and others.

Think About the Key Points from the Video Program

Each of these skills is an important part of your work with measurement and formulas:

- Knowing how to measure and what tools to use
- Taking careful and accurate measurements
- Recording measurements with appropriate labels
- Choosing the correct formula to find a measurement

The more you work with different units of measure, the more quickly you will develop good measurement skills.

WORKTIP

Whenever you use measurement on the job:

- Work carefully and accurately with the measurement tool.
- Remember the advice— measure twice; cut once.
- Be sure to include labels with your measurements; 35 pounds is a lot heavier than 35 ounces!
- Use a conversion chart if one is available.
- Choose formulas carefully.

Using English Measurement

You are probably familiar with the English measurement system, the standard units of measurement used in the United States. Here are some examples:

- Length is measured in inches, feet, yards, and miles. Tools to measure length are a ruler, yardstick, and tape measure.
- Weight is measured in ounces, pounds, and tons. Different types of scales are used to measure weight.
- Liquid measure is given in ounces, cups, pints, quarts, and gallons. To determine liquid measurements, we use measuring cups and beakers.

Use the tool pictured to select the correct measurement for each object below.

1.

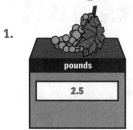

   (1)   2.5 inches
   (2)   2.5 pounds

2.

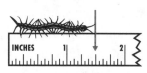

   (1) $1\frac{1}{2}$ pounds
   (2) $1\frac{1}{2}$ inches

3.

   (1) $1\frac{3}{4}$ cups
   (2) $1\frac{3}{4}$ feet

Converting English Measurements

Suppose a carpenter buys a length of wood trim that measures 46 inches. How many feet is that? To **convert** inches to feet, first find out how many inches there are in one foot. This number, 12, is called the **conversion factor.**

- To convert from a smaller unit (inch) to a larger unit (foot), you *divide* by the conversion factor.

$$12\overline{)46}$$

with quotient 3, 36 subtracted, remainder 10 ◄——— *The remainder (10) becomes the numerator of a fraction. The conversion factor (12) is the denominator. Simplify the fraction if necessary.*

46 inches = $3\frac{10}{12}$ feet, or $3\frac{5}{6}$ feet

How many ounces are equal to 2 quarts? The conversion factor is 32, because there are 32 ounces in 1 quart.

- To convert a larger unit to a smaller unit, *multiply* by the conversion factor.

2 quarts = 2 × 32 ounces = 64 ounces

Convert the following measurements. Write the conversion factor with × or ÷ to show which operation to use. (Use the chart on page 151 if you need help.)

1. 2 yards = __?__ feet
   conversion factor: __3__ __×__

2. $6\frac{1}{2}$ pints = __?__ quarts
   conversion factor: _____ __

3. 64 ounces = __?__ pounds
   conversion factor: _____ __

4. $2\frac{1}{2}$ pounds = __?__ ounces
   conversion factor: _____ __

5. 64 inches = __?__ feet
   conversion factor: _____ __

6. 13 cups = __?__ ounces
   conversion factor: _____ __

Basic Operations with English Measurement

When you are adding, subtracting, multiplying, or dividing measurements, the most important thing to remember is to work with like units.

5 yards − 4 feet = ?

You cannot subtract 4 feet from 5 yards until you convert the units of measurement so they are the same.

STEP 1: Change yards to feet or feet to yards.

1 yard = 3 feet, so 5 yards = 15 feet

STEP 2: Subtract.

15 feet − 4 feet = **11 feet**

Now try a more complex problem: 2 pounds 10 ounces + 4 pounds 15 ounces = ?

STEP 1: Add like units. 25 ounces is more than 1 pound (16 ounces), so regroup.

$$\begin{array}{r} 2 \text{ pounds } 10 \text{ ounces} \\ + 4 \text{ pounds } 15 \text{ ounces} \\ \hline 6 \text{ pounds } 25 \text{ ounces} \end{array}$$

STEP 2: Regroup. Convert 16 ounces to 1 pound; carry 1 pound to the pounds place.

25 ounces = 16 ounces + 9 ounces = 1 pound 9 ounces
6 pounds + 1 pound 9 ounces = **7 pounds 9 ounces**

Multiplying and dividing measurements require similar steps. With multiplication, you convert measurements *after* you multiply. With division, you often have to convert measurements *before* you divide.

Add, subtract, multiply, or divide as indicated. (See page 151 for more information about converting measurements.)

1. 2 pints + 32 ounces = ? pints

2. 2 pounds − 12 ounces = ? pounds

3. $10 \times 1\frac{1}{2}$ cups = ? pints

4. $2\frac{1}{2}$ feet − 10 inches = ? feet
   Hint: $\frac{1}{2}$ foot = 6 inches

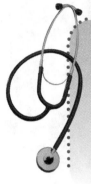

HEALTH CARE: Stephania Krolczyk is a kitchen worker at Woody Glen, an assisted living residence. This type of residence is home to elderly or disabled people who function well on their own but may need help with meals and medical care. As you know, good food and nutrition play a major role in health care. The health care industry employs thousands of kitchen workers like Stephania to help feed the sick and recovering. A major task of these health care workers is food preparation.

Below is a recipe for a dish served at Woody Glen. The recipe shows quantities of **ingredients** to serve 5 people, 10 people, 50 people, and 100 people. Knowing how many servings you need is the first step in following a recipe!

Problem Solving

As a kitchen worker, one of Stephania's jobs is to make macaroni au gratin for the residents' lunch. The job requires her to read the recipe carefully and measure ingredients accurately. Become familiar with these abbreviations. Also refer to the Reference Handbook on page 151 for additional abbreviations.

oz. = ounce   tbsp. = tablespoon   tsp. = teaspoon   lb. = pound   gal. = gallon   qt. = quart

Macaroni au Gratin portion size: 6 oz.				
Ingredients	5 servings	10 servings	50 servings	100 servings
macaroni		7 oz.	35 oz. = 2 lb. 3 oz.	4 lb. 6 oz.
water	$\frac{3}{4}$ qt.	$1\frac{1}{2}$ qt.		15 qt.
salt		$1\frac{1}{4}$ tsp.		$12\frac{1}{2}$ tsp.
margarine		5 oz.		50 oz.
flour		4 oz.		40 oz.
dry milk		1 qt.		10 qt.
pepper		$\frac{1}{4}$ tsp.		$2\frac{1}{2}$ tsp.
cheddar cheese		8 oz.		80 oz.
bread crumbs		4 oz.		40 oz.
butter		1 oz.		10 oz.

1. To make 10 servings of this dish, how much of each ingredient is needed? Draw a line on each measuring cup, or circle spoon amounts.

   a. How much water?

   b. How much flour?

   c. How much salt?

   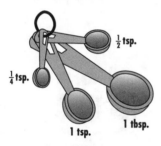

2. To make only 5 servings of this dish, how much of each ingredient is needed? Finish filling in the chart.

3. To make 50 servings of this dish, how much of each ingredient is needed? Finish filling in the chart.

WRITE IT •

Recipes often need to be increased or decreased, depending on how many servings are needed and how many servings the recipe makes.

Choose a favorite recipe, and rewrite it to change the number of servings it makes. For example, you could double the recipe or cut it in half. Be sure to use the correct measurement units. Share your revised recipe with someone to see if the reader understands them.

Using Metric Measurement

The basic units of measurement used in the metric system are the meter, which measures length; the gram, which measures weight; and the liter, which measures **capacity.** Measurements smaller or larger than these units are expressed by attaching a **prefix** (a group of letters that come before) to the word. You may remember hearing measurements such as centimeter or liter in the video program.

Here is a chart showing the different prefixes and their values.

kilo	hecto	deka	BASIC UNIT	deci	centi	milli
1000	100	10	meter gram liter	.1 (one tenth)	.01 (one hundredth)	.001 (one thousandth)

Each prefix has ten times the value of the prefix to its right on the chart. For example, one dekagram is equal to ten grams. A centiliter is equal to ten milliliters. How many meters are in a kilometer? You're correct if you said 1000.

To give you an idea of the size of each basic unit, look at the measurements given below.

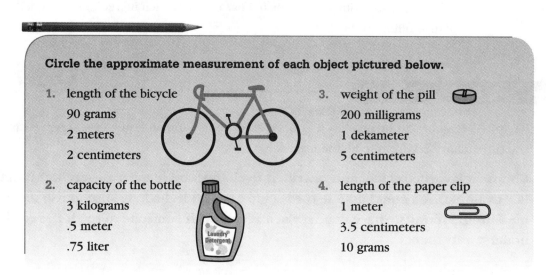

Circle the approximate measurement of each object pictured below.

1. length of the bicycle
   90 grams
   2 meters
   2 centimeters

2. capacity of the bottle
   3 kilograms
   .5 meter
   .75 liter

3. weight of the pill
   200 milligrams
   1 dekameter
   5 centimeters

4. length of the paper clip
   1 meter
   3.5 centimeters
   10 grams

Converting Metric Measurements

Metric measurements are easy to convert, since the whole system is based on tens. The conversion factor is either 10, 100, or 1000.

- When you convert from a smaller unit to a larger one, divide by the conversion factor. (There will be *fewer* meters.)   **3.5 centimeters = ? meters**
  Since there are 100 centimeters in 1 meter, the conversion factor is 100.
  $3.5 \div 100 = .035$ **3.5 centimeters = .035 meter**
- When you convert from a larger unit to a smaller one, multiply by the conversion factor. (There will be *more* milliliters.)   **1.5 liters = ? milliliters**
  Since there are 1000 milliliters in 1 liter, the conversion factor is 1000.
  $1.5 \times 1000 = 1500$ **1.5 liters = 1500 milliliters**

See page 146 for hints on multiplying and dividing by 10, 100, and 1000.

Convert the following measurements as shown. Use the chart on page 82 as needed.

1. 25.25 kilograms = _____ grams

2. 1.5 centimeters = _____ meters

3. 3400 milligrams = _____ grams

4. 2.5 liters = _____ milliliters

Basic Operations with Metric Measurement

Before you add, subtract, multiply, or divide, make sure you are working with like units. Convert units if necessary, then calculate as you would with any other numbers. For example, what is 2.5 kilograms added to 250 grams?

First, convert kilograms to grams: 2.5 kilograms = 2500 grams. Or convert grams to kilograms: 250 grams = .25 kilogram.

Then add:

	2.50 kilograms			250 grams	
	+ .25 kilogram	or	+	2500 grams	
	2.75 kilograms			2750 grams	**Both answers are correct!**

Add, subtract, multiply, or divide these metric measurements.

1. 4.9 liters × 3 = _____

2. 125 cm − 25 mm = _____

3. 400 grams + 1.5 decigrams = _____

4. 25 hectograms + 25 grams = _____

WorkSkills

MANUFACTURING: Max Holyfield is a mechanic in the machinery industry. In his job, he has to measure with great accuracy and carefully record the measurements. For example, he uses tools such as a **micrometer** or **caliper** that can measure dimensions smaller than a millimeter. Max's job requires that he have good eyesight, excellent fine **motor skills,** and an understanding of the metric system.

The metric system is the standard measurement system almost everywhere in the world except the United States. In fact, more and more businesses and industries in the United States are using the metric system to measure their products. Because it is based on multiples of ten, most people find the metric system easier to work with than the English system.

Here is a drawing of a slide caliper, sometimes called a caliper ruler. Note that it provides measurements both in inches and in millimeters. To measure, move the "jaws" of the caliper so that they are in firm contact with the surfaces of whatever is being measured.

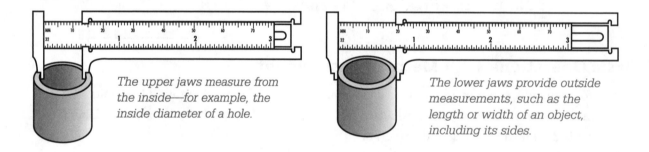

The upper jaws measure from the inside—for example, the inside diameter of a hole.

The lower jaws provide outside measurements, such as the length or width of an object, including its sides.

Then read the measurement on the caliper scale. On this caliper, millimeters are shown at the top of the ruler.

Problem Solving

On the next page, you'll find an inspection instruction sheet used in the machine tool plant where Max works. This sheet describes the necessary measurements for a metal assembly part. Use this information to answer the questions that follow. To review how to read the range, or tolerance, shown by ± in the Specification column, turn to pages 60 and 61.

Inspection Instruction Sheet • Northwest Metalworks, Inc.		
Characteristic	**Specification**	**Measurement Tool**
Weight	280–320 grams	weight scale
Thickness	5.5 mm ± .5 mm	calipers
Pin holes/splits	none allowed	visual
Length	14.5 mm ± .5 mm	calipers
Width	10 mm ± 1.5 mm	calipers
Date code	present and correct	visual

Decide whether each part pictured below meets the specifications in the chart by reading the caliper or scale measurements. Circle YES or NO.

Example: YES ⟨NO⟩

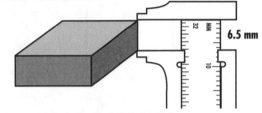

Specification range for thickness:

$5.5 - .5 = 5.0$ and $5.5 + .5 = 6.0$

Does the part meet the given specifications?

No, the measurement is outside the range.

1. YES
   NO

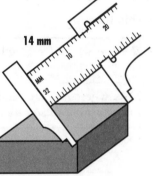

3. YES
   NO

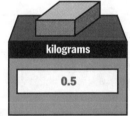

Hint: A kilogram is 1000 times as heavy as a gram.

2. YES
   NO

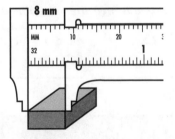

4. YES
   NO

COMMUNICATE •

Which system of measurement do you think is easier to use—English or metric? What are some of your reasons?

Find a partner, or imagine that you are speaking before a group. Your job is to convince someone that the system of measurement you prefer is the *only* system that should be used in our country. Write down points to support your ideas. Use examples from your own work and everyday life.

Formulas and Problem Solving

A formula is a statement that shows the constant (unchanging) relationship between values. Math formulas express relationships by using variables. If we know a value for every variable but one, we can **substitute** numbers in place of the variables we know and then use the formula to solve for the unknown value.

For example, when you need to find the boundary, or **perimeter,** of a square, use the formula $P = 4s$. P stands for perimeter and s for the length of one side.

Suppose you know that one side of a square is 5 centimeters long. By substituting 5 in place of s, you'll find the perimeter (P) of that square.

$P = 4s$ ⟵ *When a number and variable are side by side,*

$P = (4)(s)$ *the operation is multiplication. Side-by-side parentheses also mean multiplication.*

s

$P = (4)(5)$

$P = 20$ ⟵ **The perimeter of the square is 20 cm.**

Here are some common formulas and what they stand for:

To find:		Use this formula:
perimeter of a rectangle	w / l	$P = 2l + 2w$, where l = length and w = width
area of a square	s	$A = s \times s$, where A = area and s = length of side *(Area is measured in square units, or units^2.)*
area of a rectangle	w / l	$A = l \times w$
volume of a cube	s	$V = s \times s \times s$ *(Volume is measured in cubic units, or units^3.)*
volume of a rectangular solid	h / w l	$V = l \times w \times h$, where h = height

Substitute the given values into the correct formula to solve for the unknown variables.

1. What is the volume of a cube when $s = 2$ in.? $V = $ _____ cu. in.

   $V = s^3 = s \times s \times s = 2 \times 2 \times 2 = $ _____ cu. in.

2. What is the area of a rectangle, when $l = 2$ ft. and $w = 5$ ft.? $A = $ _____ sq. ft.

3. What is the perimeter of a square, when $s = 1$ mi.? $P = $ _____ mi.

4. What is the perimeter of a rectangle when $l = 10$ yd. and $w = 6$ yd.? _____ yd.

Solving Problems Using Formulas

Now you know how to substitute numbers for the variables in a formula. In life and on the job, however, you won't always be told which formula to use. This is where your problem-solving skills come in.

What formula does a carpet layer use to decide how much carpet she'll need to cover a floor? When you measure the surface of something, you are finding area. Area is measured in square units, or units². Choose which area formula to use by looking at the shape of the area. In this case, she would use $A = lw$.

```
┌──────────────────────────────┐
│                              │
│         Family Room          │
│                              │
└──────────────────────────────┘
```

What formula does a construction worker use to find out how much cement is needed to fill a rectangular base? When you are figuring out capacity, or how much something holds, you are measuring volume. Volume is measured in cubic units, or units³, because three dimensions are involved: length, width, and height. In this case, he would use $V = lwh$.

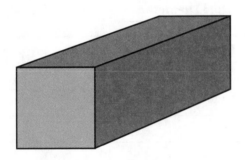

Choose the correct formula, then solve each problem below. Use the chart on page 86 to help you.

1. How much water will a plastic container hold if it measures 10 cm long, 8 cm wide, and 2 cm deep? Hint: The shape is a rectangular solid. _____ cm³

2. How long is a fence that surrounds a square field that has sides of 25 yards each? _____

3. A landscaper needs to put weed killer on a yard that measures 100 yards long by 50 yards wide. How much area does the weed killer need to cover? _____

4. A machinist cuts a piece of metal that measures 3.5 mm in length and 2.5 mm in width. What is the area of this piece? _____

CONSTRUCTION: As you've seen, measurement plays a big role in the construction industry. Formulas can help workers determine area, perimeter, and volume of squares and rectangles. This kind of information is useful whether you are building, covering a floor, cutting metal, or constructing a fence.

On the next two pages, you'll be focusing on shapes and formulas that we have not worked with yet—the circle and its area and perimeter, as well as the cylinder and its volume. You'll see how the measurement of circles is based on the value π, which represents a special characteristic of circles.

Problem Solving

As a carpenter's assistant, Gina needs to be familiar with different kinds of drills, drill bits, and hole measurements. Look at the information below.

Drills and Hole Diameters	
Drill	**Used for Holes with a Diameter of:**
twist drill	$\frac{1}{16}" - \frac{1}{2}"$
power spade drill	$\frac{3}{8}" - 1\frac{1}{2}"$
hole saw	$1\frac{1}{2}" - 6"$
fly cutter	$\frac{1}{2}" - 8"$

FORMULAS:

Circumference (perimeter) of a circle: $C = \pi d$, where $\pi = 3.14$ and $d =$ **diameter**

diameter

Area of a circle: $A = \pi r^2$, where $r =$ **radius,** which is $\frac{1}{2}$ the diameter

radius

Volume of a cylinder: $V = \pi r^2 h$, where $h =$ height

h *radius*

The diagrams below indicate the size of holes to be cut.

- Before you calculate circumference or area, change each fraction to its equivalent decimal. (See page 150 for equivalent values.)
- Use a calculator to perform any calculations.
- Round all decimals to the nearest hundredth.

Example:

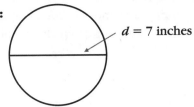

$d = 7$ inches

a. What type of drill should be used to cut this hole? **fly cutter**

b. What will be the circumference of the circle? $C = 3.14 \times d = 3.14 \times 7 = $ **21.98 in.**

c. What will the area of the circle be? $A = 3.14 \times 3.5^2 = 3.14 \times 12.25 = $ **38.47 sq. in.**

1. a. What types of drill can be used to cut this hole?

_____ or _____

$d = 1\frac{5}{8}$ inches

b. What will be the circumference of the circle? _____

c. What will the area of the circle be? _____

2. a. What type of drill should be used to cut this hole? _____

$d = \frac{1}{4}$ inches

b. What will be the circumference of the circle? _____

c. What will the area of the circle be? _____

3. a. What types of drill can be used to cut this hole?

_____ or _____ or _____

$d = 1\frac{1}{2}$ inches

b. What will be the circumference of the circle? _____

c. What will the area of the circle be? _____

TECH TIP ....

Pi (π) is the constant relationship between the diameter and circumference of a circle. The circumference of any circle is always a little more than three times the length of its diameter. When we say that the value of pi is 3.14, we are actually using an approximation. What is the value of π?

Press the π key on your calculator. Why do you think we use the estimate 3.14 as the value of π instead of its true value?

Review

CONSTRUCTION: Pablo is a carpenter. Before he accepts a job, he first meets with the customer to talk about what needs to be done. He then draws up an estimate of what he will charge the customer. To come up with this estimate, Pablo takes measurements, chooses materials, checks prices, and estimates the time and number of workers needed to do the job well.

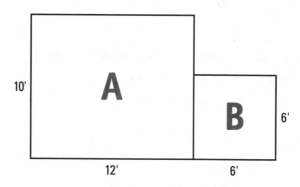

Above is a floor plan Pablo drew for building an outdoor deck. Use this information and the formulas you learned in this program to answer the questions.

1. What is the area of section A of the deck?

   (1)   22 ft.
   (2)   22 sq. ft.
   (3)   44 sq. ft.
   (4)   120 sq. ft.

2. Below section B of the deck, Pablo needs to pour 6 inches of gravel. How many cubic feet of gravel will he need?

   (1) $12\frac{1}{2}$
   (2)   18
   (3)   24
   (4)   216

3. To build a railing around the entire deck, Pablo needs to figure out the perimeter. What is the perimeter of the deck? Hint: Use only the outside measurements. To find lengths you do not know, add and subtract lengths you know.

   (1)   108 ft.
   (2)   56 ft.
   (3)   50 ft.
   (4)   40 ft.

The chart below lists some of the materials needed to build the deck. Use the chart to answer the questions that follow. The size of a piece of lumber is described by its depth times its width times its length. Therefore, a 2" × 4" × 8' board is 2 inches deep, 4 inches wide, and 8 feet long.

Materials	Total Needed	Hours of Labor
concrete mix	4 cubic feet	2.5
2" × 6" × 10' boards	40 linear feet	2
2" × 6" × 8' boards	72 linear feet	3.5
2" × 4" × 10' boards	280 linear feet	8.5
2" × 4" × 3' railing posts	30 linear feet	1
2" × 4" × 3' railings	52 linear feet	1.5
#10d galvanized nails	8 pounds	
$\frac{1}{2}$" lag bolts, 4" long	18 each	

4. How many 2" × 6" × 10' boards are needed for this project? Hint: Look at the total needed for the listed material.

   (1) 40
   (2) 30
   (3) 10
   (4) 4

5. How many total *yards* of 2" × 6" × 8' lumber are needed?

   (1) 24
   (2) 48
   (3) 72
   (4) 216

6. How many total *inches* of railing posts are needed?

   (1) 2.5
   (2) 30
   (3) 360
   (4) 3600

7. How many total hours of labor does Pablo estimate it will take to do the concrete work, install all the boards, and put up the railing posts and railings?

    (1) 15.5
    (2) 19
    (3) 21.5
    (4) 24.5

8. If Pablo paid an assistant $7.80 per hour to mix and pour the concrete, how much would the assistant be paid for the job?

    (1) $19.50
    (2) $10.50
    (3) $7.80
    (4) $3.12

9. If 2" × 6" × 8' boards cost $5.77 each, how much will Pablo pay for the 2" × 6" × 8' boards he needs? Hint: How many 8' boards will he need?

    (1) $414.44
    (2) $51.93
    (3) $46.16
    (4) $5.77

10. How much will Pablo spend on 2" × 4" × 10' boards if they cost $4.65 a piece?

    (1) $46.50
    (2) $130.20
    (3) $260
    (4) $1302

Trends and Predictions: Graphs and Data

The video program you are about to watch will show how **data** is collected and used in the workplace. When we gather a lot of numerical information and present it in an organized way, we call it data. Data can represent everything from the number of people on a payroll to the average size of a pinhole drilled into a piece of metal.

You'll also see in this video program how data can be presented visually. Employers and employees both use pictures or drawings to explain and understand the data better. Have you ever heard the saying "A picture is worth a thousand words"? This video will show examples of more effective ways to pass on information than by simply using words.

As you watch the program, pay attention to how people describe things using data and graphs. Try to see when and why the information is easy to understand.

OBJECTIVES

In this lesson, you will work with these math concepts and skills to do workplace tasks:

1. Reading bar graphs, circle graphs, line graphs, and **spreadsheets**

2. Drawing conclusions based on data

3. Making predictions based on data

4. Finding **averages** of groups of numbers

Sneak Preview

This exercise previews some of the concepts from Program 24. After you answer the questions, use the Feedback on page 95 to help you set your learning goals.

MANUFACTURING: NBS Industries encourages its employees to stay informed about what is happening in their workplace. One way employees do this is by reading the employee bulletin board in the break room. On this board, workers and managers post information about meetings, safety issues, and company policies.

Two items posted in the NBS employee lounge are Graphs A and B below. Use this information to answer the questions that follow.

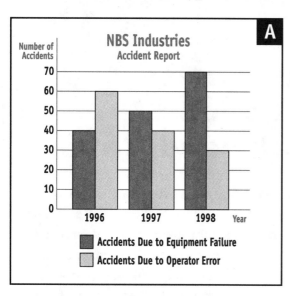

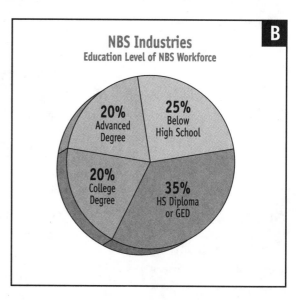

1. How many accidents caused by equipment failure were reported at NBS in 1996?

   (1) 40
   (2) 50
   (3) 60

2. What percent of the NBS workforce has a high school diploma or more?

   (1) 25%
   (2) 35%
   (3) 75%

3. In what year were the reported accidents due to operator failure the highest?

   (1) 1996
   (2) 1997
   (3) 1998

4. Which of the following statements is supported by Graph A?

    (1) Equipment has been getting safer in the years since 1996.
    (2) The number of operator-caused accidents declined from 1996 to 1997 and from 1997 to 1998.
    (3) Accidents caused by equipment failure are more serious than those caused by operator error.

5. Which of the following statements is supported by Graph B?

    (1) Most NBS employees have at least a high school diploma or a GED.
    (2) All people who work at NBS are well educated.
    (3) More NBS employees have advanced degrees than college degrees.

6. What was the average number of operator-error accidents over the three-year period shown in Graph A?

    (1) 130
    (2) 43
    (3) 30

Feedback

- If you got all of the questions right . . .   you have a foundation for working with graphs and data. Concentrate on how data and graphs are used in many other ways in the video program.

- If you missed question 1 or 2 . . .   you need to work on reading graphs.

- If you missed question 3 . . .   you need to learn more about comparing and using data.

- If you missed question 4 or 5 . . .   concentrate on developing your data analysis skills, such as drawing conclusions and making inferences.

- If you missed question 6 . . .   pay special attention to how to find averages.

Answers for Sneak Preview:
1. Choice (1)   2. Choice (3)   3. Choice (3)   4. Choice (1)   5. Choice (2)   6. Choice (2)

Vocabulary for *Trends and Predictions: Graphs and Data*

averages	numbers that are typical in sets of numbers
axis	the vertical or horizontal reference line on a graph
census	an official count of an entire group, such as all the people in a nation
continuous	not ending
data	a collection of numbers that gives information about a subject
key	information that helps interpret a graph
mean	the average found by dividing a total of numbers by the quantity of numbers in the set
population	an entire group to be studied statistically
productivity	the amount of usable product; often measured in terms of hours of labor or cost of materials
sample	a representative portion of a population
spreadsheets	tables of rows and columns that organize and present data
statistics	the collection, organization, and interpretation of data
trends	general directions, courses, or tendencies

PBS LiteracyLink®

Now watch Program 24.

After you watch, work on:
- pages 97–112 in this workbook
- Internet activities at www.pbs.org/literacy

AFTER you WATCH

Trends and Predictions: Graphs and Data

On the following pages, you will learn more about the graph and data skills discussed in the video program you have just watched. You'll also have the opportunity to practice these skills and others.

Think About the Key Points from the Video Program

Each of these skills is an important part of working with graphs and data:

- Understanding how data is collected and organized
- Reading bar, circle, and line graphs
- Finding averages
- Understanding spreadsheets
- Drawing conclusions based on data
- Seeing **trends** in data

The more you work with data and graphs, the more you will see how useful these tools are in your work.

WORKTIP

Whenever you see a chart or graph on the job:

- Try to understand the overall purpose of the graph or chart.
- Read all labels shown.
- Look carefully at the data before you draw any conclusions.

What Is Data?

The term data refers to a collection of numbers that gives information about a subject. Here are some examples of data:

- The United States government collects data about its citizens through a yearly **census** in which people are asked questions about their age, education, employment, family status— even pet ownership.
- Most workplaces keep data about their income, expenses, employees, and productivity.
- Newspapers and television provide data on surveys that they have conducted on everything from people's opinion of their elected officials to what kind of toothpaste people prefer.

As you saw in the video program, this data can be presented in many ways.

Bar Graphs

A bar graph is one example of how data can be organized and presented. As with any kind of graph or chart, pay attention to the title and all labels of the graph. What data is being presented in the bar graph below?

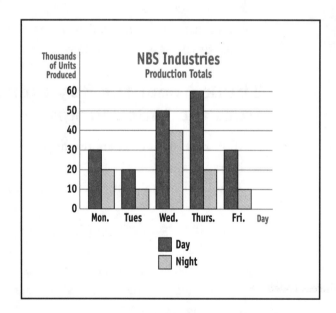

- The graph title tells you that the data represents production totals at NBS Industries.
- The vertical **axis** (line running top to bottom) labels tell you that the numbers represent *thousands* of units produced. That means that a bar reaching the "20" mark indicates 20,000 units produced.
- The horizontal axis (line running left to right) labels tell you that the data is presented by *days of the week*, Monday through Friday.
- The **key** tells you that dark green bars represent the *day shift* and light green bars represent the *night shift.*

Use the bar graph on page 98 to answer these questions.

1. How many units were produced during the day shift on Tuesday? _____
2. How many units were produced in all on Friday, including both shifts? _____
3. Which shift on which day produced the most units? _____
4. How many more units were produced during the day shift than during the night shift on Monday? _____

Finding Averages

When people work with data, it is often useful to find an average, such as the **mean** value. The mean value is a number that is approximately in the middle of all the values. What is the mean in this group of numbers: 35, 50, 72, 75?

To find the mean, follow these steps:

1. Add up all the numbers in the set of data.

$$35 + 50 + 72 + 75 = 232$$

There are four numbers being added in this set.

2. Divide this total by the number of items in the set of data.

$$232 \div 4 = 58$$

58 is the mean for this set of data.

Use these steps and the graph on page 98 to find the average number of units produced per shift at NBS on Monday.

1. Add up all the numbers in the set of data.

$$30,000 + 20,000 = 50,000$$

There are two numbers being added in this set.

2. Divide this total by the number of items in the set of data.

$$50,000 \div 2 = 25,000$$

25,000 is the average number of units produced per shift at NBS on Monday.

Find these mean values based on the bar graph on page 98. Remember that the graph shows *thousands* of units.

1. What is the average number of units produced in the day shifts during this week? _____
2. What is the average number of units produced in the night shifts during this week? _____
3. What is the average number of units produced *per day* during the last three days of the week? (Include both shifts.) _____

SERVICE: Spark's Electronics, like other modern businesses, stays competitive by constantly collecting information. The employees and managers at Spark's have to keep up with the new information that is continually becoming available to them. Fortunately for the employees at Spark's and other businesses, computers can store, organize, update, and print out this ever-changing data.

One data analysis tool that most businesses use in one form or another is the spreadsheet. Spreadsheets display data in the form of rows and columns set in a table or chart. On a computerized or electronic spreadsheet, when a change is made in one square, or cell, the computer *automatically* calculates and organizes any necessary changes in other cells.

Problem Solving

Lu is a sales assistant for Spark's. One of her jobs is to record sales information on an electronic spreadsheet at the end of each week. Every Friday, Lu uses a computer program and inputs the dollars in sales made by each employee. She also inputs what the sales manager provided as a goal for each employee.

On the next page you will find a sample of the spreadsheet Lu uses. Column A lists the salespeople's names, Column B lists actual sales dollars, Column C lists goal dollars, and Column D lists percent of goal reached. Each row is numbered and includes the name of each salesperson.

Begin inputting information onto the spreadsheet on page 101. The directions below tell you how to do this. Do not enter dollar signs with dollar amounts.

1. Martinez sold $5400 in electronics this week. Record this amount in cell B2. (Note: B2 is the cell where Column B and Row 2 come together.)

2. Samuelson sold $1200 in electronics this week. Record this amount in cell B3.

3. The sales manager calls to tell you that Martinez's goal for the week was $6000 and Samuelson's goal was $2000. Record this data in the correct cells in Column C.

<table>
<tr><td colspan="5">SPARK'S ELECTRONICS
Sales Figures—Week of 1/5</td></tr>
<tr><td></td><td>A</td><td>B</td><td>C</td><td>D</td></tr>
<tr><td>1</td><td>Salesperson</td><td>$ in Sales</td><td>$ Goal</td><td>% of Goal Reached</td></tr>
<tr><td>2</td><td>Martinez</td><td></td><td></td><td>90%</td></tr>
<tr><td>3</td><td>Samuelson</td><td></td><td></td><td>60%</td></tr>
<tr><td>4</td><td>Hauser</td><td></td><td></td><td>93.75%</td></tr>
<tr><td>5</td><td>Hughes</td><td></td><td></td><td>17.5%</td></tr>
<tr><td>6</td><td>Chung</td><td></td><td></td><td>100%</td></tr>
<tr><td>7</td><td>Russell</td><td></td><td></td><td>125%</td></tr>
<tr><td>8</td><td>Team Average</td><td></td><td></td><td>75.81%</td></tr>
</table>

4. Once there is data in Columns B and C, the computer *automatically* calculates the values for Column D. The computer has already been given the formula $\frac{B}{C}$, or B ÷ C, to calculate the value to be placed in Column D. Use a calculator to check the values in Cell D2 and Cell D3.

Fill in each cell of the spreadsheet using the information below.

Hauser and Russell each sold $3750 in electronics during the week of 1/5. Hauser's goal was $4000, while Russell's goal was only $3000. Hughes and Chung each had a goal of $8000 in sales for the week. Chung actually sold $8000 in electronics, but Hughes was sick for three days and his total sales came to $1400.

5. Fill in the team average $ in Sales and $ Goal in cells B8 and C8. (Remember, to find the average, add up total dollars and divide by 6, which is the number of salespeople. Round the averages to the nearest cent.)

6. Finally, use your calculator to check the figures in Column D. See page 150 if you need help changing decimals to percents.

WRITE IT

Spreadsheets and graphs show data in an easy-to-read format. However, they are often accompanied by a written or oral report that helps people interpret the data. This report can highlight interesting pieces of the data or can summarize the data and explain why it is useful.

Write a brief report to your supervisor based on either the bar graph on page 98 or the filled-in spreadsheet above. Tell what you find interesting or important about the data. Write at least two paragraphs.

Data and Statistics

What do **statistics** like this really tell us? "34% of Americans are satisfied with the U.S. Postal Service." Did someone go out and ask all 250 million citizens of the United States what they thought of the postal service? No.

The study of statistics makes it possible to learn about a group of people, places, or things (a **population**) by looking at information about a smaller part of that group (a **sample**).

In this case, a survey was conducted, and a very carefully chosen group of Americans was asked about postal service satisfaction. The sample of people surveyed was considered representative of the larger population. In other words, they had the same characteristics as the larger population.

What does "34% of Americans" actually mean? As you learned earlier, 34% means 34 out of 100. Because the sample was representative, we can conclude that out of every 100 Americans, 34 of them are satisfied with the postal service.

If there are 250,000,000 Americans, how many are satisfied with the postal service? (Review pages 66–67 if you need to.)

$$34\% \text{ of } 250,000,000 =$$
$$.34 \times 250,000,000 = \textbf{85,000,000, or 85 million}$$

Change the percent to a decimal.

Use the statistics given in the problems below to answer the questions.

1. Supervisors at your company state that 15% of packages sent out last week were incorrectly labeled. You estimate that about 900 packages were sent out. Approximately how many were incorrectly labeled? _____

2. A survey showed that 45% of city households paid for their own trash removal. If there are 14,000 households in the city, how many pay for their own trash removal? _____

3. Of the one hundred circuit boards inspected, the quality-control team found three to be defective. Based on this percentage, how many defective boards would you expect to find in today's production of 10,000 units? _____

4. If 40% of the state university's 750 employees want better benefits, how many of the employees want better benefits? _____

Circle Graphs

A very common way to show percents visually is to use a circle graph, sometimes called a pie chart. A cirlce graph represents a whole such as 1, 100% or $1. In the example below, what percent of shipments went to Germany in 1997?

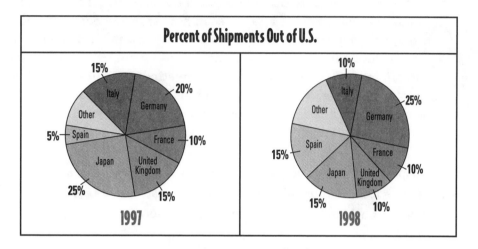

Percent of Shipments Out of U.S.

1997

1998

You are correct if you determined that **20%** of shipments went to Germany. Therefore, if there were 800 shipments during 1997, how many of those went to Germany?

20% of 800 =

.20 × 800 = **160 shipments to Germany**

Answer these questions based on the circle graphs above.

1. **a.** Between 1997 and 1998, did the percent of shipments to Japan go up or down?
   b. By how much?

2. If there were 1100 shipments in 1998, how many shipments went to Spain?

3. **a.** Of the 800 shipments in 1997, what percent went to "other" countries (those not named on the graph)?
   b. How many shipments went to these "other" countries?

Write two statements describing data from the graphs.

Example: The percent of shipments to France remained the same from 1997 to 1998.

4. _____

   _____

5. _____

   _____

MANUFACTURING: In many manufacturing plants, employees need to be able to gather statistics, understand them, and present them in an organized way. You've already seen how spreadsheets and circle graphs are used to work with data. Many computer programs in the workplace can use the data from a spreadsheet to create a circle graph. In this lesson, you'll practice creating circle graphs without the help of a computer, but keep in mind that you can also do many of the tasks described below with a computer graphics program.

To create a circle graph that shows exact percentages, you would need special tools such as a compass and protractor. For your work here, simply estimate the approximate size of each "piece of the pie." To help guide you, remember these equivalents:

100% = 1 whole

50% = $\frac{1}{2}$

$33\frac{1}{3}\%$ = $\frac{1}{3}$

25% = $\frac{1}{4}$

Problem Solving

Use the data provided to complete each circle graph. Remember to use labels similar to those you saw on page 103. For some, you may have to figure out one of the percents.

1. Twenty-four percent of the aluminum plates produced at XYZ Corporation this week were sent back for refining. Forty-nine percent were shipped out on schedule, and twenty-seven percent of the aluminum plates were scrapped.

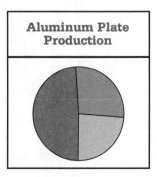

Aluminum Plate Production

2. Six percent of people surveyed said they rarely followed safety rules on the job. Fifteen percent said they sometimes followed safety rules, and fifteen percent said they usually followed safety rules. Sixty-four percent of those surveyed said they always followed safety rules.

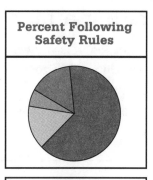

Percent Following Safety Rules

3. From every one of LaMont's paychecks, 30% of his income is taken out in taxes, and 5% goes into his retirement fund. He has 1% deducted for charity, and the rest is deposited directly into his checking account at Midland Bank. (Remember that the whole circle equals 100%.)

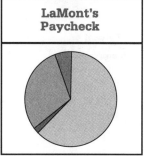

LaMont's Paycheck

4. Of every 100 pages printed at Waverton Press, 79 are usually in excellent condition, 15 are smudged or soiled, and 6 are too light.

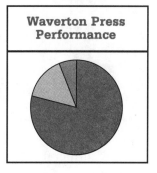

Waverton Press Performance

TECH TIP ••

Most calculators have a percent key (%) that makes it easy to find percentages. Find the percent key on your calculator, and follow the steps below to find what percent 18 is of 90.

1.	Enter the number that represents the part of the whole.	`1` `8` → `18.`
2.	Press the division key.	`÷` → `18.`
3.	Enter the number that represents the whole.	`9` `0` → `90.`
4.	Press the percent key.	`%` → `0.9`
5.	Press the equals key. (Note that on some calculators, you can skip step 5.) **18 is 20% of 90.**	`=` → `20.`

Use a calculator to find these percents. Round answers to the nearest tenth.

1. What percent of 120 is 15?

2. What percent of 3500 is 250?

Reading a Line Graph

A line graph is another way to organize and present data. Like a bar graph, a line graph uses vertical and horizontal axes, data points, and labels to show data visually. On a line graph, however, data points are connected with a **continuous** line. On the graph below, determine what the unemployment rate was in 1990. First find 1990 on the horizontal axis. Move straight up to the data line. Now move straight across to the vertical axis and see what value you are on.

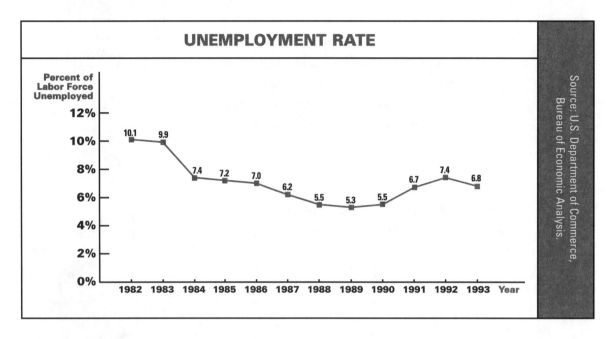

You are correct if you found that the 1990 unemployment rate was **5.5%.**

Use the line graph above to answer the following questions.

1. What was the unemployment rate in 1982? _____

2. In what year shown was the unemployment rate the lowest? _____

3. Was the 1987 unemployment rate higher or lower than the rate in 1993?

   _____

4. In how many of the years shown was the unemployment rate below 6%?

   _____

Seeing Trends in Data

The horizontal axis of a line graph usually represents time—either weeks, months, or years. By connecting data points in one continuous line, you are able to see how something changes over time. In other words, you can see **trends**—general direction or movement.

What trends do you notice looking at the unemployment graph above?

You are correct if you noticed that the unemployment rate went down between 1982 and 1989, then began to rise again.

Use the graph below to answer the following questions. Be sure to use the key provided with the graph.

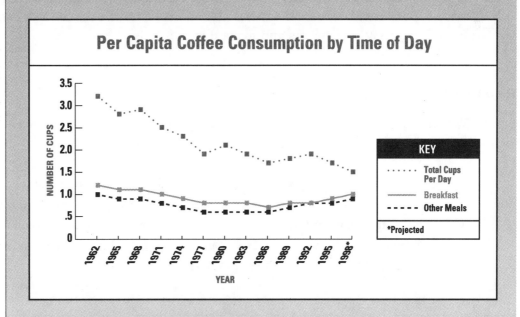

1. Which of these statements is true according to the graph?

   (1) Total coffee consumption went down between 1962 and 1971.
   (2) Total coffee consumption rose between 1971 and 1977.

2. What trend do you notice about coffee consumption at breakfast time?

   (1) Coffee consumption at breakfast time greatly decreased between 1962 and 1995.
   (2) Coffee consumption at breakfast time declined slightly between 1962 and 1995.

3. During which 3-year period was the change in total coffee consumption the greatest?

   (1) 1962–1965
   (2) 1986–1989
   (3) 1989–1992

4. Approximately how many cups of coffee were consumed per day per person at breakfast in 1995?

   (1) about one and a half
   (2) about 1
   (3) about one-half

RETAIL: Like other food service workers in restaurants, Celia Prinz has to understand data from a variety of sources. In her job at Chez Joy, Celia has researched pricing trends for beef by reading charts and graphs, and she reads food industry magazines that publish the results of surveys. Many times, Celia uses data to help her draw conclusions and make decisions.

Problem Solving

When you draw a conclusion, you use all the information you have as well as your own experience, and you come up with a new understanding.

Based on her training and experience in handling food, Celia knows that certain foods must be kept cold so that germs and bacteria do not grow. Several times a day, Celia checks the temperature of the foods on the salad bar and the temperature of the walk-in freezer unit. She must draw conclusions based on what she knows about food storage and the data from the graph below.

To draw a conclusion, follow these steps:

- What information is provided on the graph?
- What facts about food and quantity do I already know?
- What new understanding do I have when I put this information together?

Use the information from the graph to answer the questions on page 109.

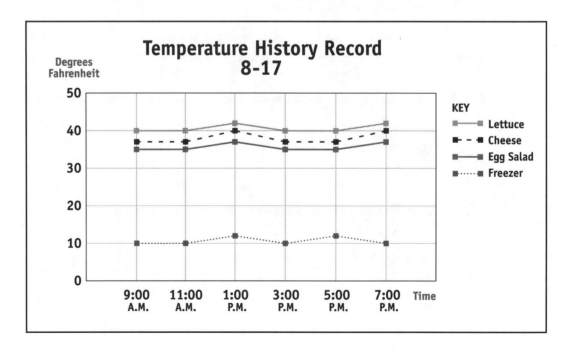

1. Food temperatures rise as the quantity decreases. Which of the following conclusions can you draw using this information and data from the graph?

   (1) From 11 A.M. to 1 P.M. and from 5 P.M. to 7 P.M., there is less food on the salad bar than at other times.
   (2) Lettuce is a more popular food on the salad bar than egg salad and cheese.
   (3) The temperature of the cheese is higher than the egg salad temperature in the morning but lower in the afternoon.

2. Policy states that egg salad should never reach a temperature higher than 35 degrees. Which of the following can you conclude?

   (1) The egg salad that was served on August 17 was acceptable.
   (2) It is unhealthy to serve egg salad on a hot day.
   (3) The egg salad should have been removed after 11 A.M.

3. The temperature of the walk-in freezer increases when employees open the door frequently. Celia's manager asks her to come up with a plan to keep the freezer temperature around or below 10 degrees. Choose the best plan.

   (1) Try to limit the number of times the freezer door is opened between 11:00 and 1:00 and between 3:00 and 5:00.
   (2) Lower the freezer temperature to 8 degrees so that, even when employees open the door, the temperature won't go above 10 degrees.
   (3) Turn the freezer thermostat down to 10 degrees and leave it there.

4. Celia knows from a food science workshop that the temperature at which some foods freeze is 32 degrees. Which of the following can she conclude based on this information and on the graph?

   (1) All the items in the freezer melt after 11:00 A.M.
   (2) The cheese on the salad bar is frozen.
   (3) The lettuce, cheese, and egg salad on the salad bar are not frozen.

COMMUNICATE

Suppose you are to give a report to the management of a coffee manufacturer. Use the data from the graph on page 107 to convince them that they should consider manufacturing another beverage in addition to coffee. First make a list of your main points, then prepare an oral argument.

Your oral report should be about 3 minutes long.

Review

Data and statistics are useful when a business is trying to improve **productivity,** which is really just getting the maximum benefit from the work being done. Businesses collect data about time, money, and materials, then use this information to make decisions.

Below is a chart showing work sampling observations in a manufacturing plant. Every 20 seconds, a quality-control worker puts a tally mark in the column that describes the action being performed by the worker.

For example, if at one reading, the worker is walking to the assembly table, a tally mark is placed in the "Walk" column. If 20 seconds later the worker is waiting for a part to come down the conveyor belt, a tally mark is put in the "Wait" column.

Notice that 100 readings are taken during each shift. ‖‖ represents 5 tally marks. One tally mark is shown as / .

Shift	Main Work	Handle	Walk	Pack	Wait
6:00–10:00 A.M.	‖‖ ‖‖ ‖‖ ‖‖ ‖‖ ‖‖ ‖‖ ‖‖ ‖‖ ‖‖ ‖‖ ‖‖	‖‖ ///	‖‖ ‖‖ /	‖‖ ‖‖ ///	‖‖ ///
10:00 A.M.–2:00 P.M.	‖‖ ‖‖ ‖‖ ‖‖ ‖‖ ‖‖ ‖‖ ‖‖ ‖‖ ‖‖ /	‖‖ ‖‖ ‖‖	‖‖ /	‖‖ ‖‖ ‖‖	‖‖ ‖‖ ///
2:00–6:00 P.M.	‖‖ ‖‖ ‖‖ ‖‖ ‖‖ ‖‖ ‖‖ ‖‖ ///	‖‖ ‖‖ ‖‖ ‖‖ //	‖‖	‖‖ ‖‖ ////	‖‖ ‖‖ ‖‖ /
6:00–10:00 P.M.	‖‖ ‖‖ ‖‖ ‖‖ ‖‖ ‖‖ ‖‖ ‖‖	‖‖ ‖‖ ‖‖ ‖‖ ////	///	‖‖ ‖‖ ‖‖ ‖‖ ///	‖‖ ‖‖
Line Averages					

1. Add up the tally marks in each cell, and record the percentages on the spreadsheet below. A computer has started your work for you.

A Shift	B Main Work	C Handle	D Walk	E Pack	F Wait
1 6:00–10:00 A.M.	60%	8%	11%	13%	8%
2 10:00 A.M.–2:00 P.M.	51%	15%	6%	15%	13%
3 2:00–6:00 P.M.	43%		5%		16%
4 6:00–10:00 P.M.	40%		3%		10%
5 Line Averages					

2. Which bar graph below best represents the data showing percent of time spent on "Main Work" for all four shifts?

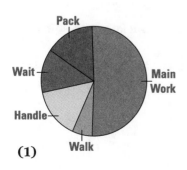

(1)

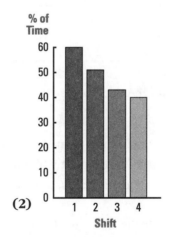

(2)

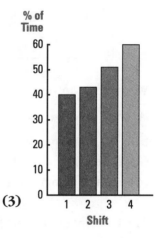

(3)

3. Which circle graph below best represents the data showing time spent during the 10:00 A.M.–2:00 P.M. shift?

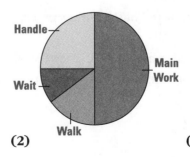

(1)

(2)

(3)

4. Draw a line graph showing the data for the percent of time spent walking during the four shifts. Be sure to include all labels.

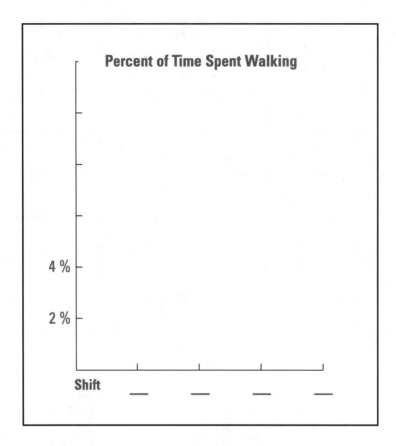

5. What trend do you notice from the data in the "Walk" column?

    (1) More time is spent walking as the day goes on.
    (2) Walking time does not change much from shift to shift.
    (3) The earlier the shift, the more time spent walking.
    (4) As the amount of walking time decreases, the amount of waiting time decreases.

6. The time spent in "Main Work" is the most productive time. Which of the following conclusions can you draw based on the data provided?

    (1) To raise productivity, the company should close down after 2:00 P.M.
    (2) Third and fourth shift employees could learn about productivity from the employees of earlier shifts.
    (3) More people are employed in the earlier two shifts than in the later two shifts.

7. Suppose this company added a 10:00 P.M.–2:00 A.M. shift. Assuming the trend would continue, what percent of time would be spent on main work?

    (1) less than 40%
    (2) between 40% and 50%
    (3) more than 50%

Skills Review

The following questions are based on the skills you learned in video programs 20 through 24 and this book. Answer the questions, check your answers, and fill in the evaluation chart on page 124.

Questions 1–3 are based on this employee wage scale.

# of shifts	1	2	3	4	5
# of hours	7	14	_____	28	35
total pay	$35.35	$ _____	$106.05	$141.40	$176.75

1. Based on this wage scale, how much would an employee earn by working 14 hours?

    (1) $49.35
    (2) $60.20
    (3) $70.70
    (4) $80.70

2. How many hours are there in 3 shifts?

    (1) 24
    (2) 21
    (3) 20
    (4) 18

3. What is this worker's hourly pay?

    (1) $5.05
    (2) $7.00
    (3) $10.50
    (4) $17.00

Questions 4–10 are based on this store transfer invoice.

Product	Quantity	Units	Unit Cost	Total Cost
SOUTHBURY FARMS STORE Store Transfer Invoice Date Shipped:_____				
whole wheat bread	20	cases		$285.60
Souper Supper	10	cases	$11.00	$110.00
large eggs		dozen	$.69	$17.25
Empire apples	26	pounds	$.98	
whole chickens	55	pounds	$.59	$32.45
fresh-squeezed orange juice	60	half gallons	$1.49	$89.40
russet potatoes	8	cases	$8.90	$71.20

4. What is the unit cost of a case of whole wheat bread?

   (1) $571.20
   (2) $20.00
   (3) $17.60
   (4) $14.28

5. How many dozens of large eggs were transferred?

   (1) 12
   (2) 25
   (3) 45
   (4) 70

6. There are 24 cans of Souper Supper in every case. How many *cans* were transferred?

   (1) 10
   (2) 20
   (3) 200
   (4) 240

7. *Estimate* the total cost of the Empire apples.

   (1) $1.00
   (2) $10.00
   (3) $26.00
   (4) $28.00

8. The average weight of a whole chicken is 2.5 pounds. *Approximately* how many chickens were transferred?

   (1) 22
   (2) 34
   (3) 55
   (4) 138

9. How many *quarts* of orange juice were transferred?

   (1) 30
   (2) 60
   (3) 120
   (4) 140

10. Twenty-five percent of the total cost of russet potatoes goes to the potato farmer. How much money does the farmer get from these potatoes?

   (1) $17.80
   (2) $22.25
   (3) $44.50
   (4) $284.80

Questions 11–13 refer to the following pattern. It gives the proper measurements for large sweatpants.

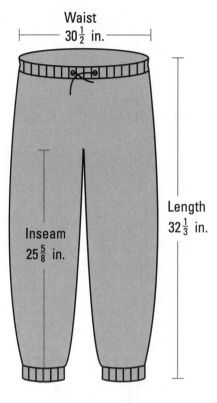

Waist
30½ in.

Length
32⅓ in.

Inseam
25⅝ in.

11. A bolt of cloth has 40 feet remaining. What is the greatest number of lengths ($32\frac{1}{3}$ inches) that can be cut from it?

   (1) one
   (2) two
   (3) fourteen
   (4) fifteen

12. The tolerance measurement for the sweatpants inseam is $\pm\frac{1}{2}$ inch. Is a pair of sweatpants with an inseam of $25\frac{1}{8}$ inches acceptable?

   (1) yes
   (2) no

13. Small sweatpants are $1\frac{3}{4}$ inches smaller in the waist than a large pair. How many inches is the small waistband?

   (1) $32\frac{1}{4}$
   (2) $30\frac{1}{2}$
   (3) $29\frac{3}{4}$
   (4) $28\frac{3}{4}$

Questions 14–16 refer to the following chart used by machinists.

Decimal Equivalents of Drill Sizes	
Drill Number	Diameter, in inches
80	0.0135
78	0.016
76	0.02
74	0.0225
72	0.025
70	0.028
68	0.031
66	0.033
64	0.036

14. As the diameter gets larger, the drill number gets smaller. What number drill would measure 0.0292?

    (1) 77
    (2) 71
    (3) 69
    (4) 68

15. What is the difference in diameter (in inches) between a #64 drill and a #68 drill?

    (1) .067
    (2) .005
    (3) .025
    (4) .05

16. Is a drill with a 0.0145-inch diameter smaller or larger than #78?

    (1) smaller
    (2) larger

Questions 17–20 refer to the following quality-control time chart.

Shift	Main Work	Handle	Walk	Pack	Wait
A 6:00–10:00 A.M.	2 hours	1.5 hours	.25 hour	.25 hour	1 hour
B 10:00 A.M.–2:00 P.M.	2.1 hours	1 hour	.5 hour	.75 hour	.65 hour
C 2:00–6:00 P.M.	2.1 hours	.75 hour	.25 hour	.9 hour	0 hours
D 6:00–10:00 P.M.	2 hours	.5 hour	.5 hour	.1 hour	.9 hour

17. How many hours were spent walking between 6:00 A.M. and 10:00 P.M.?

    (1) .25
    (2) .75
    (3) 1
    (4) 1.5

18. How much more time, in hours, was spent on main work than packing during Shift C?

    (1) 3
    (2) 1.2
    (3) 1.1
    (4) .9

19. What fraction of the day (6:00 A.M.–10:00 P.M.) was spent packing?

    (1) $\frac{1}{4}$
    (2) $\frac{1}{6}$
    (3) $\frac{1}{8}$
    (4) $\frac{1}{16}$

20. What percent of Shift A was spent handling?

    (1) 10
    (2) 10.5
    (3) 25
    (4) 37.5

Questions 21–23 refer to the graph below.

21. In which month are the actual number of sick days twice the number of projected sick days?

    (1) January
    (2) March
    (3) May
    (4) July

22. How many more actual sick days per employee were there in March than in May?

    (1) one
    (2) two
    (3) three
    (4) four

23. Which of the following statements is true based on the graph?

    (1) The actual number of sick days per employee is usually lower than projected.
    (2) The projected number of sick days per employee is higher in summer than in winter.
    (3) The projected number of sick days per employee gets lower as the weather gets warmer.

Questions 24–26 refer to the following sketch of an aluminum plate being cut in a metal working shop.

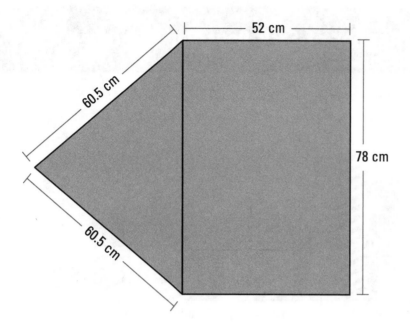

24. What is the perimeter of the entire metal plate?

    (1) 151 cm
    (2) 220 cm
    (3) 203 cm
    (4) 303 cm

25. What is the perimeter of the triangular figure, in *meters?*

    (1) 1.99
    (2) 19
    (3) 19.9
    (4) 199

26. What is the area, in square *meters,* of the rectangular figure? (Hint: Convert the measurements to meters *before* multiplying.)

    (1) 0.4056
    (2) 26
    (3) 40.56
    (4) 260

Questions 27–29 refer to the following carpenter's drawing.

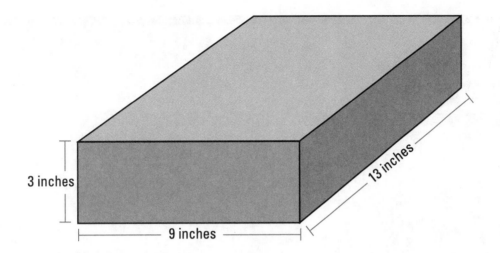

27. How many *feet* long is the block of wood?

    (1) 13
    (2) 1.3
    (3) $1\frac{1}{12}$
    (4) 1

28. What is the volume, in cubic inches, of the block?

    (1) 401
    (2) 351
    (3) 149
    (4) 25

29. The carpenter cuts $\frac{1}{3}$ foot from the width of the block. How many inches wide is the remaining block?

    (1) 4
    (2) 5
    (3) 6
    (4) 7

Questions 30–32 refer to the following car sales graph.

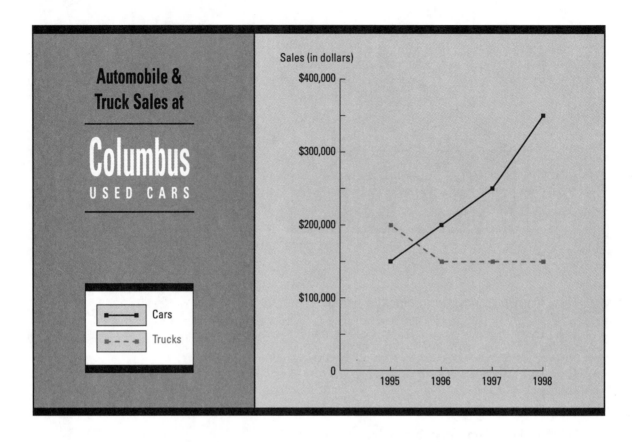

30. In what year did car sales first exceed truck sales?

    (1) 1995
    (2) 1996
    (3) 1997
    (4) 1998

31. Which of the following statements describes the trend in truck sales between 1995 and 1998?

    (1) Sales fell slightly during 1995 and remained steady through 1997.
    (2) Sales rose steadily throughout the time period.
    (3) Sales rose slightly during 1995, then dropped off until 1998.
    (4) Sales fell slightly in 1996, then continued to rise.

32. Which of the following statements is true based on the graph?

    (1) Car sales exceeded truck sales by $50,000 every year.
    (2) Truck sales fell $100,000 between 1995 and 1998.
    (3) Car sales rose $200,000 between 1995 and 1998.
    (4) Car sales rose $400,000 between 1995 and 1998.

Skills Review Answers

1. (3) $70.70
2. (2) 21
3. (1) $5.05
4. (4) $14.28
5. (2) 25
6. (4) 240
7. (3) $26.00
8. (1) 22
9. (3) 120
10. (1) $17.80
11. (3) fourteen
12. (1) yes
13. (4) $28\frac{3}{4}$
14. (3) 69
15. (2) .005
16. (1) smaller
17. (4) 1.5
18. (2) 1.2
19. (3) $\frac{1}{8}$
20. (4) 37.5
21. (4) July
22. (1) one
23. (3) The projected number of sick days per employee gets lower as the weather gets warmer.
24. (4) 303 cm
25. (1) 1.99
26. (1) 0.4056
27. (3) $1\frac{1}{12}$
28. (2) 351
29. (2) 5
30. (1) 1995
31. (1) Sales fell slightly during 1995 and remained steady through 1997.
32. (3) Car sales rose $200,000 between 1995 and 1998.

Skills Review Evaluation Chart

Circle the question numbers that you answered correctly. Then fill in the number of questions you got correct for each program lesson. Find the total number correct, and review the lessons you had trouble with.

Program Lesson	Question Number	Number Correct/Total
20: *Number Sense* Working with Place Value; Grouping, Sorting, and Using Patterns; Estimation and Number Sense	1, 2, 3	____/3
21: *Solving Problems* Adding and Subtracting, Multiplying and Dividing, Estimating and Problem Solving	4, 5, 6, 7, 8	____/5
22: *Fractions, Decimals, and Percents* Reading Decimals, Understanding and Comparing Fractions, Understanding Proportion and Percent	10, 11, 12, 13, 14, 15, 16, 17, 18, 19, 20	____/11
23: *Measurements and Formulas* Using English Measurement, Using Metric Measurement, Formulas and Problem Solving	9, 24, 25, 26, 27, 28, 29	____/7
24: *Trends and Predictions: Graphs and Data* Reading Bar, Circle, and Line Graphs; Understanding Spreadsheets; Drawing Conclusions, Seeing Trends, and Finding Averages	21, 22, 23, 30, 31, 32	____/6
	Total	____/32

WHAT YOUR SCORE MEANS

If you got 29–32 correct: You have strong math skills and a good understanding of how to effectively apply those skills on the job.

If you got 26–28 correct: Try to figure out why you got each answer wrong. Review the sections for the items you missed to improve your workplace math skills.

If you got 22–25 correct: You need to improve your workplace math skills. Review any program in which you missed more than one item.

If you got less than 22 correct: You need to review the basic math skills in each program. By reviewing the programs and revisiting the exercises in this book, you can gain the knowledge and skills you need to be effective when working with math in the workplace.

Answer Key

Working with Place Value, page 18

2. 1040

3. 17,402

4. 20,560

Comparing Values, page 19

1. 8287 < 9043

2. 747 > 738

3. 22,000 = 22,000

4. 77 < 114

5. 801,332 > 99,999

6. 1055 > 1008

7. Answers will vary. The number on the left should be *greater than* the number on the right.

8. Answers will vary. The number on the left should be *less than* the number on the right.

Ordering Numbers, page 19

1. 33, 38, 41, 101

2. 9, 57, 75, 95

3. 1127, 1125, 1119, 978

4. 210, 201, 109, 104

WorkSkills, pages 20–21
See answers below.

Teller Balancing Record

Date _____

Ending Balance	9,033	00
Beginning Balance	12,500	00
Took to Vault		
Got from Vault		
Working Fund Adj.	⟨3,467	00⟩

Total Checks for Deposits	14,421	21
Total Checks Disbursed		
Cash Over		
Cash Short		
Working Fund Adj.	⟨3,467	00⟩
Net Cash-Net	10,954	21
ADJUSTMENTS		
Marked Money		
100s	5,700	00
50s	350	00
20s	2,000	00
10s	450	00
5s	500	00
1s	33	00
TOTAL	9,033	00

Communicate, page 21

Answers will vary. This example shows the kinds of numbers you might have included in your description. How many numbers were you able to include?

I am 48 years old, and I have been married for 30 years. I have 5 children, ages 18, 20, 24, 27, and 28. I've completed 11 years of school, and I work 3 different jobs during the week. I spend 10 hours cleaning offices, 25 hours working in a childcare center, and 20 hours at the assembly plant downtown. I am 5'4" tall. I live at 1142 Washington Avenue, and my phone number is 402-555-7212.

Grouping, Sorting, and Using Patterns, page 22

1. $3\frac{1}{2}$ hours
2. $7\frac{1}{2}$ hours
3. 6 employees
4. 10 shifts (5 days × 2 per day)

Sorting and Grouping Numbers, page 23

1. a. screens under 6 feet tall: VQ901, VQ934, VQ121

   b. screens 6 feet tall and over: VQ022, VQ207

2. a. 48-inch-wide screens: VQ121, VQ207

   b. screens that are not 48 inches wide: VQ901, VQ934, VQ022

3. a. $\frac{1}{2}$-inch gauge screens: VQ022, VQ121

   b. screens that are greater than $\frac{1}{2}$-inch gauge: VQ901, VQ934, VQ207

4. a. screens less than 42 inches wide: VQ901, VQ934

   b. screens 42 inches wide or greater: VQ022, VQ121, VQ207

Using Patterns, page 23

1. 4 shifts
2. 12 hours
3. $175
4. 24 hours
5. 8 shifts
6. $350

WorkSkills, page 25

1. J
2. B
3. A
4. K
5. C
6. G
7. H
8. C
9. H
10. D

Write It, page 25

Answers will vary. Be sure you described your pattern thoroughly and provided details when necessary. Did you notice that all the left-hand page numbers in this book are even numbers? You can also say that they are all divisible by 2.

Estimation and Number Sense, page 26

1. 130
2. 10
3. 10
4. 50
5. 30
6. 260
7. 100
8. 40

Estimating with Easy Numbers, page 27

2. 70 + 100 + 10 = 180 rods
3. 30 × 10 = 300 minutes
4. $150 − $40 = $110
5. 200 ÷ 10 = 20 inches

Estimating with Money, page 27

1. $17
2. $987
3. $25
4. $12
5. $102
6. $10
7. $802
8. $1021

WorkSkills, pages 28–29

2. $47 \approx $50

3. $282 \approx $280

4. $114 \approx $110

5. $106 \approx $110

6. wood step, Type III, 6-foot ladder

7. aluminum extension, Type I, 28-foot ladder

8. aluminum extension, Type II, 28-foot ladder

Read It, page 29

Answers will vary. You may have circled advertisements that talked about low prices or good value. Most people want to spend less yet get something of good quality. Did some of your ads use descriptive words such as *exciting, new, lowest price ever,* or *unbeatable?* These words and phrases often get people's attention. Did you think about why a store might price something $4.99 instead of $5.00? Even though they are only a penny apart, $4.99 may seem much less than $5.00 if people round down to $4 instead of up to $5.

Review, pages 30–32

1. a. 1200

   b. 2100

   c. 5340

   d. 2480

2. Granny Smith apples, zucchini squash, oranges, nectarines

3. celery sticks, romano salad, papayas, Bartlett pears, Granny Smith apples, oranges

4. a. Storage Area C

   b. Refrigeration Unit #2

   c. Refrigeration Unit #1

   d. Storage Area A

5. See answers below.

Description	Estimated Total Amount
Cortland apples	$80
Red Delicious	$40
Granny Smith	$270
Golden Delicious	0
Papayas	$20
Pineapple	0
Zucchini squash	$50
Butternut squash	$40
Buttercup squash	$10
Carrot shredded	$10
Celery sticks	$10
Romano salad	$10
Oranges	$200
Avocados	$50
Nectarines	$400
Bartlett pears	$60
Fresh figs	0

PROGRAM 21: SOLVING PROBLEMS

Adding and Subtracting, page 38

1. 2225
2. 1693
3. 88
4. 89,353
5. 869
6. 932
7. 1211
8. 669

Adding and Subtracting with Regrouping, page 39

1. 1672
2. 8082
3. 1213
4. 733
5. 1420
6. 1790

Adding and Subtracting Money, page 39

1. $476.78
2. $4460.68
3. $150.66
4. $926.25
5. $317.79
6. $4798.43
7. $109.08
8. $1115.67

WorkSkills, pages 40–41

See answers below.

Check No. 4507

Server: _____ Date: _____

eggs benedict	$3.25
side bacon	1.45
2 eggs over easy / toast	1.95
lg. orange juice	1.15
2 coffees	1.50
TOTAL DUE	**$9.30**

Change back from $20: _____ $10.70

Check No. 4508

Server: _____ Date: _____

side sausage	$1.55
pancake platter	3.95
2 muffins	1.80
bagel/cream cheese	1.15
sm orange juice	.85
waffle w/strawberries	2.75
2 sides bacon	2.90
1 milk	.95
3 coffees	2.25
1 tea	.65
TOTAL DUE	**$18.80**

Change back from $20: _____ $1.20

Check No. 4509

Server: _____ Date: _____

3 eggs scrambled/toast	$2.95
ham	1.55
mushroom/cheese omelet	3.05
lg. orange juice	1.15
cold cereal	.95
fruit plate	2.05
4 coffees	3.00
TOTAL DUE	**$14.70**

Change back from $20: _____ $5.30

Check No. 4510

Server: _____ Date: _____

3 X 3 Special	$3.95
pancakes	2.45
French toast	2.15
bagel/butter	.80
2 soft-boiled eggs/toast	1.95
2 sides bacon	2.90
1 coffee	.75
2 teas	1.30
2 milks	1.90
TOTAL DUE	**$18.15**

Change back from $20: _____ $1.85

Communicate, page 41

Answers will vary. When you add up the costs, be sure to keep digits lined up correctly. Remember that careless or sloppy work will almost always produce an incorrect total. Try using a calculator to check your work whenever possible.

Multiplying and Dividing, page 42

1. 84
2. 378
3. 6175
4. 735
5. 9143
6. 25,350

Dividing, page 43

1. 14
2. 161
3. 82
4. 365
5. 30
6. 114

Multiplying and Dividing with Money, page 43

1. $140.88
2. $308.00
3. $41.09
4. $35.50
5. $353.75
6. $12.19

WorkSkills, page 45

See answers below.

Read It, page 45

Answers will vary. If you couldn't find the "coverage" information on paint cans and household cleaners, be sure you look at the smaller print at the bottom of the labels.

Estimating and Problem Solving, page 46

1. $13 + 22 = 35; 1300 + 2200 = 3500$
2. $43 - 12 = 31; 4300 - 1200 = 3100$
3. $19 + 22 = 41; 19,000 + 22,000 = 41,000$
4. $67 - 35 = 32; 6700 - 3500 = 3200$
5. $95 - 23 = 72; 95,000 - 23,000 = 72,000$
6. $41 + 85 = 126; 4100 + 8500 = 12,600$
7. $29 - 11 = 18; 2900 - 1100 = 1800$
8. $20 + 10 = 30; 20,000 + 10,000 = 30,000$

Compatible Pairs, page 47

1. $550 \div 5 = 110$
2. $240 \div 6 = 40$
3. $810 \div 9 = 90$
4. $600 \div 3 = 200$

Estimation and the Calculator, page 47

1. correct
2. 458
3. 91,736
4. 4576
5. 11,040
6. correct
7. 2112
8. correct

A	B	C	D	E
Job	Room Measurements (length × width)	Tile Needed	Type/Cost of Tile (per sq. ft.)	Number of Cases Needed
121 Larks St.	8' × 9'	72 sq. ft.	slate/$1.19	7
79A Bellingham Dr.	13' × 11'	143 sq. ft.	quarry tile/$1.77	13
9205 Main	27' × 19'	513 sq. ft.	ceramic/$1.58	47
33 Pine Rd.	18' × 16'	288 sq. ft.	vinyl/$.59	27

See answers below.

BLOOM'S Sporting Goods
RECONCILIATION SHEET

DATE: _____   COMPLETED BY: _____   REVIEWED BY: _____

Beginning Drawer Balance:	$ 485.50	
(add) Total Sales:	~~$ 98.64~~	980.64
(add) Gift Certificates Redeemed:	$ 100.00	
(subtract) Total Refunds:	$ 48.97	
(subtract) Coupons Redeemed:	$ 28.00	
END-OF-DAY TOTAL:	~~$ 607.17~~	$1489.17

Communicate, page 49

Your answer may differ from the one below. Notice how the person who wrote this answer decided to speak to the co-worker first and ask questions instead of placing blame.

If I checked my co-worker's calculations and found a mistake, I would first go to the co-worker and discuss the situation. I would make sure he or she agreed that there was a mistake. Then we would try to correct it together. If it was a serious mistake and I felt that my co-worker might do it again, I would tell him or her that we should discuss it with our supervisor.

This is how I'd like the situation to be handled if I made a mistake. Also, this would help me maintain a good relationship with my co-worker.

1–3. See answers below.

Petty Cash Report

Date: _4/12_

Beginning total: $ _595.00_ (A)

Cash on hand: $ _392.74_

Receipts: $ _202.26_

Total: $ _595.00_ (B) (should equal A)

---

4. $7.55

5. See answers below.

Petty Cash Report

Date: _4/12_

Beginning total: $ _595.00_ (A)

Cash on hand: $ _400.29_

Receipts: $ _194.71_

Total: $ _595.00_ (B) (should equal A)

PROGRAM 22: FRACTIONS, DECIMALS, AND PERCENTS

Reading Decimals, page 58
2. 21.014
3. 105.6
4. 62.010

Comparing Decimals, page 58
1. 10.9
2. 4.511
3. 5.72
4. 85.06

Adding and Subtracting Decimals, page 59
1. 26.25
2. 3.348
3. 21.525
4. 13.705
5. 52.94
6. 6.34

Multiplying and Dividing Decimals, page 59
1. 14.446
2. 0.432
3. 324.435
4. 21.37
5. 45.57
6. 0.56

WorkSkills, pages 60–61
1. a. 1.75
   b. 2.005
   c. 1.07
   d. 3.014
   e. 2.129
2. smallest: 9:00
   largest: 8:30
3. .35 mm
4. smallest: 1.8
   largest: 2.8 mm
5. a. 8:00
   b. 9:30

Write It, page 61
Answers will vary. However, be sure you have included some of the ideas in the paragraph below.

Our money system and the decimal system are similar because they both use a decimal point to separate whole numbers from numbers smaller than one. The smallest coin in the money system is the penny, which is one hundredth of a dollar. However, the decimal system includes parts much smaller than that.

Understanding and Comparing Fractions, page 62
1. $\frac{5}{6}$
2. $\frac{1}{4}$
3. $\frac{7}{9}$
4. $\frac{3}{4}$
5. $\frac{3}{4}$
6. $\frac{11}{12}$

Adding and Subtracting Fractions, page 63
1. $\frac{5}{8}$
2. $\frac{4}{9}$
3. $\frac{4}{5}$
4. $\frac{5}{8}$
5. $\frac{17}{12} = 1\frac{5}{12}$
6. $\frac{6}{10} = \frac{3}{5}$

Multiplying and Dividing Fractions, page 63
1. $\frac{2}{15}$
2. 90
3. $\frac{1}{2}$
4. 2
5. $\frac{8}{15}$
6. $\frac{10}{27}$

WorkSkills, page 65
1. $\frac{3}{4} \times 90 = 67\frac{1}{2}$
2. $\frac{1}{2} \times \frac{3}{4} = \frac{3}{8}$
3. $\frac{1}{3} \times 72 = 24$
4. $\frac{1}{2} \times \frac{1}{2} = \frac{1}{4}$
5. $\frac{1}{2} \times 400 = 200$

Tech Tip, page 65

To change $\frac{7}{8}$ to a decimal using a calculator, press 7, then $\div$, then 8, then $=$. The display will read 0.875. The fraction $\frac{3}{5}$ written as a decimal is 0.6. Enter 3, then divide by 5.

Understanding Proportion and Percent, page 66

1. $\frac{2}{7} = \frac{4}{a}$; $2a = 4 \times 7$; $2a = 28$; $a = 14$
2. $\frac{3}{4} = \frac{b}{100}$; $300 = 4b$; $b = 75$
3. $\frac{x}{10} = \frac{14}{5}$; $5x = 140$; $x = 28$
4. $\frac{1}{y} = \frac{9}{27}$; $27 = 9y$; $y = 3$
5. $\frac{x}{3} = \frac{14}{6}$; $6x = 42$; $x = 7$
6. $\frac{2}{9} = \frac{6}{a}$; $2a = 54$; $a = 27$

Writing Percents, page 67

1. 70% $\frac{7}{10}$ .7
2. 25% $\frac{1}{4}$ .25
3. 37.5% $\frac{3}{8}$ .375
4. 75% $\frac{3}{4}$ .75

Solving Percent Problems, page 67

1. 25%
2. 750
3. 75
4. 88

WorkSkills, page 68

See answers below.

Weekly Bagel Production and Throwaway Sheet

WEEK OF: _October 20_

Flavor	Monday	Tuesday	Wednesday	Thursday	Friday	TOTAL
plain	220 baked / 11 thrown away	300 baked / 20 thrown away	300 baked / 10 thrown away	220 baked / 22 thrown away	560 baked / 28 thrown away	1600 baked / 91 thrown away
onion	150 baked / 30 thrown away	120 baked / 10 thrown away	200 baked / 25 thrown away	220 baked / 11 thrown away	400 baked / 20 thrown away	1090 baked / 96 thrown away
sesame	140 baked / 7 thrown away	240 baked / 8 thrown away	250 baked / 25 thrown away	100 baked / 4 thrown away	200 baked / 12 thrown away	930 baked / 56 thrown away
salt	170 baked / 34 thrown away	200 baked / 6 thrown away	220 baked / 22 thrown away	180 baked / 10 thrown away	340 baked / 17 thrown away	1110 baked / 89 thrown away
garlic	220 baked / 11 thrown away	220 baked / 11 thrown away	220 baked / 11 thrown away	220 baked / 11 thrown away	220 baked / 11 thrown away	1100 baked / 55 thrown away
cinnamon raisin	500 baked / 25 thrown away	200 baked / 10 thrown away	300 baked / 15 thrown away	220 baked / 11 thrown away	620 baked / 31 thrown away	1840 baked / 92 thrown away
TOTAL	1400 baked / 118 thrown away	1280 baked / 65 thrown away	1490 baked / 108 thrown away	1160 baked / 69 thrown away	2340 baked / 119 thrown away	7670 baked / 479 thrown away

Percent Throwaways						
Flavor	**Monday**	**Tuesday**	**Wednesday**	**Thursday**	**Friday**	**TOTAL**
plain	5 %	7 %	3 %	10 %	5 %	6 %
onion	20 %	8 %	13 %	5 %	5 %	9 %
sesame	5 %	3 %	10 %	4 %	6 %	6 %
salt	20 %	3 %	10 %	6 %	5 %	8 %
garlic	5 %	5 %	5 %	5 %	5 %	5 %
cinnamon raisin	5 %	5 %	5 %	5 %	5 %	5 %
TOTAL	8 %	5 %	7 %	6 %	5 %	6 %

Read It, page 69

Answers will vary. If you had trouble finding percents in the newspaper, try these places: any advertisement that might list a "percent off" sale, a chart or graph that gives information about a community, or an article that tells the results of a survey. Remember that percents can be expressed by the symbol % as well as by the word *percent*.

Review, pages 70–72

1. (3) 39

$$24 \times 1\frac{5}{8} =$$
$$24 \times \frac{13}{8} = 39$$

2. (1) 17

$$40 \div 2\frac{1}{4} =$$
$$40 \div \frac{9}{4} =$$
$$40 \times \frac{4}{9} = \frac{160}{9} = 17\frac{7}{9}$$

17 pairs can be made, with $\frac{7}{9}$ yd. left over.

3. (2) $3.00

$2\frac{7}{8}$ yd. is about 3 yards.

$.99 per yard is about $1.00 per yard.

$3 \times \$1.00 = \$3.00$

4. back seam too short
   inseam too short

5. waist too narrow
   leg hem too wide

6. leg hem too narrow

7. waist too narrow

8. back seam too short

PROGRAM 23: MEASUREMENTS AND FORMULAS

Using English Measurement, page 78

1. (2) 2.5 pounds
2. (2) $1\frac{1}{2}$ inches
3. (1) $1\frac{3}{4}$ cups

Converting English Measurements, page 79

1. 6 feet; conversion factor: 3 ×
2. $3\frac{1}{4}$ quarts; conversion factor: 2 ÷
3. 4 pounds; conversion factor: 16 ÷
4. 40 ounces; conversion factor: 16 ×
5. $5\frac{1}{3}$ feet; conversion factor: 12 ÷
6. 104 ounces; conversion factor: 8 ×

Basic Operations with English Measurement, page 79

1. 4 pints
2. 1 pound 4 ounces = $1\frac{1}{4}$ pounds
3. $7\frac{1}{2}$ pints
4. $1\frac{2}{3}$ feet

WorkSkills, pages 80–81

1. a.

b.

c.

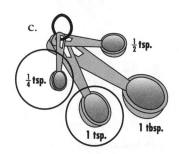

2–3. See answers below.

	Macaroni au Gratin portion size: 6 oz.			
Ingredients	5 servings	10 servings	50 servings	100 servings
macaroni	$3\frac{1}{2}$ oz.	7 oz.	35 oz. = 2 lb. 3 oz.	4 lb. 6 oz.
water	$\frac{3}{4}$ qt.	$1\frac{1}{2}$ qt.	$7\frac{1}{2}$ qt. = 1 gal. $3\frac{1}{2}$ qt.	15 qt.
salt	$\frac{5}{8}$ tsp.	$1\frac{1}{4}$ tsp.	$6\frac{1}{4}$ tsp.	$12\frac{1}{2}$ tsp.
margarine	$2\frac{1}{2}$ oz.	5 oz.	25 oz. = 1 lb. 9 oz.	50 oz.
flour	2 oz.	4 oz.	20 oz. = 1 lb. 4 oz.	40 oz.
dry milk	1 pint	1 qt.	5 qt. = 1 gal. 1 qt.	10 qt.
pepper	$\frac{1}{8}$ tsp.	$\frac{1}{4}$ tsp.	$1\frac{1}{4}$ tsp.	$2\frac{1}{2}$ tsp.
cheddar cheese	4 oz.	8 oz.	40 oz. = 2 lb. 8 oz.	80 oz.
bread crumbs	2 oz.	4 oz.	20 oz. = 1 lb. 4 oz.	40 oz.
butter	$\frac{1}{2}$ oz.	1 oz.	5 oz.	10 oz.

Write It, page 81

Answers will vary. For example, to double a recipe, be sure each ingredient is multiplied by the same factor (2).

Using Metric Measurement, page 82

1. 2 meters
2. .75 liter
3. 200 milligrams
4. 3.5 centimeters

Converting Metric Measurements, page 83

1. 25,250 grams
2. .015 meter
3. 3.4 grams
4. 2500 milliliters

Basic Operations with Metric Measurement, page 83

1. 14.7 liters
2. 122.5 cm or 1225 mm
3. 400.15 grams or 4001.5 decigrams
4. 2525 grams or 25.25 hectograms

WorkSkills, page 85

1. Yes
   Specification range for length:
   $14.5 - .5 = 14.0$ and $14.5 + .5 = 15.0$
   Yes, the measurement 14 mm is within the range.
2. No
   Specification range for width:
   $10.0 - 1.5 = 8.5$ and $10.0 + 1.5 = 11.5$
   No, the measurement 8 mm is outside the range.
3. No
   Specification range for weight:
   280 – 320 grams; 0.5 kilograms = 500 grams
   No, the measurement 0.5 kilogram is outside the range.
4. No
   Specification range for weight:
   280 – 320 grams
   No, the measurement 30.0 grams is outside the range.

Communicate, page 85

Answers will vary. There is no correct answer to the English-vs.-metric debate. Some people think the English system is better because more people (in the United States) are familiar with it. Others like the easier computation in the metric system. Whichever method you chose, be sure you gave specific reasons to support your point of view.

Formulas and Problem Solving, page 86

1. 8 cu. in.
2. 10 sq. ft.
3. 4 mi.
4. 32 yd.

Solving Problems Using Formulas, page 87

1. 160 cm^3
2. 100 yd.
3. 5000 sq. yd.
4. 8.75 mm^2

WorkSkills, pages 88–89

1. a. hole saw or fly cutter
   b. 5.10 in.
   c. 2.07 sq. in.
2. a. twist drill
   b. .79 in.
   c. .05 sq. in.
3. a. power spade drill, hole saw, or fly cutter
   b. 4.71 in.
   c. 1.77 sq. in.

Tech Tip, page 89

The exact value of π goes on indefinitely. The value for π on a calculator is usually 3.141592654. We use 3.14 because it is a close approximation, and it is easier to work with.

Review, pages 90–92

1. (4) 120 sq. ft.

   10' × 12' = 120 sq. ft.

2. (2) 18

   6' × 6' × $\frac{1}{2}$' = 18 cu. ft.

3. (2) 56 feet

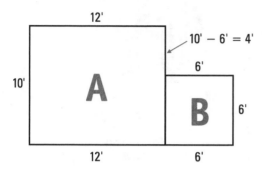

4. (4) 4

   40 ÷ 10 = 4

5. (1) 24

   72 ÷ 3 = 24

6. (3) 360

   30 × 12 = 360

7. (2) 19

   2.5 + 2 + 3.5 + 8.5 + 1 + 1.5 = 19

8. (1) $19.50

   2.5 × $7.80 = $19.50

9. (2) $51.93

   72 ÷ 8 = 9

   9 × $5.77 = $51.93

10. (2) $130.20

    280 ÷ 10 = 28

    28 × $4.65 = $130.20

PROGRAM 24: TRENDS AND PREDICTIONS: GRAPHS AND DATA

Bar Graphs, page 99

1. 20,000
2. 40,000
3. Thursday, day shift
4. 10,000

Finding Averages, page 99

1. 38,000
2. 20,000
3. 70,000

WorkSkills, page 101

1–5. See answers below.

6. The percentages in Column D are correct.

	A	**B**	**C**	**D**
	Salesperson	$ in Sales	$ Goal	% of Goal Reached
1				
2	Martinez	5400.00	6000.00	90%
3	Samuelson	1200.00	2000.00	60%
4	Hauser	3750.00	4000.00	93.75%
5	Hughes	1400.00	8000.00	17.5%
6	Chung	8000.00	8000.00	100%
7	Russell	3750.00	3000.00	125%
8	Team Average	$3916.67	$5166.67	75.81%

SPARK'S ELECTRONICS
Sales Figures—Week of 1/5

Write It, page 101

Here is a sample report about the spreadsheet on page 101. Answers will vary but should include some of the same ideas.

Overall, the sales team reached about 76% of its goal the week of January 5, averaging about $4000 in sales. Russell surpassed her goal of $3000 by $750, and Chung was the top dollar salesperson with $8000 sold. Sales ranged from $1200 to $8000 among the six salespeople.

Hughes achieved only 17.5% of his goal due to three days of illness. Only two salepeople reached their goal, but two others reached 90% or better.

Data and Statistics, page 102

1. 135
2. 6300
3. 300
4. 300

Circle Graphs, page 103

1. a. down

   b. 10%
2. 165
3. a. 10%

   b. 80
4. Answers will vary. Example: The percent of shipments to Japan dropped from $\frac{1}{4}$, or 25%, in 1997 to 15% in 1998.
5. Answers will vary. Example: The percent of shipments going to Spain increased from 5% in 1997 to 15% in 1998.

WorkSkills, pages 104–105

1.
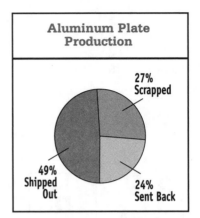

2.
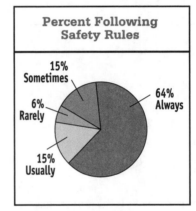

3.
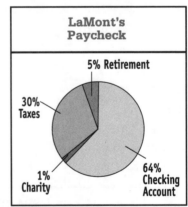

4.
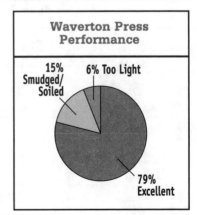

Tech Tip, page 105

1. 12.5%
2. 7.1%

Reading a Line Graph, page 106

1. 10.1%
2. 1989
3. lower
4. three

Seeing Trends in Data, page 107

1. (1)
2. (2)
3. (1)
4. (2)

WorkSkills, page 109

1. (1)
2. (3)
3. (2)
4. (3)

Communicate, page 109

Answers may vary. Your list of main points for your oral report should include the following:

- The total cups of coffee consumed per day has steadily decreased.
- The amount of coffee consumed at meals has remained steady with no significant increases.
- If the trend in total coffee consumption continues, the total cups consumed per day will decline even more.

Review, pages 110–112

1.

A Shift	B Main Work	C Handle	D Walk	E Pack	F Wait
1 6:00– 10:00 A.M.	60%	8%	11%	13%	8%
2 10:00 A.M.– 2:00 P.M.	51%	15%	6%	15%	13%
3 2:00– 6:00 P.M.	43%	22%	5%	14%	16%
4 6:00– 10:00 P.M.	40%	24%	3%	23%	10%
5 Line Averages	48.5%	17.25%	6.25%	16.25%	11.75%

2. (2)
3. (1)

4.

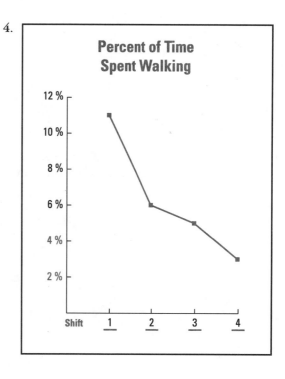

5. (3)
6. (2)
7. (1)

Glossary

alphanumeric: combining letters and numbers, as in a label on items in a store, business, or warehouse

approximate: close, but not exact

area: the size of a surface

averages: numbers that are typical in sets of numbers

axis: the vertical or horizontal reference line on a graph

bank teller: a person who works directly with customers and their withdrawals from and deposits to the bank

beginning balance: the amount of cash issued to a bank teller at the beginning of the day

borrowing: regrouping numbers when subtracting

calculations: math processes—such as adding, subtracting, multiplying, and dividing—carried out to solve a problem

caliper: an instrument used to measure internal (inside) and external (outer) dimensions

capacity: the maximum amount that can be held or contained

carry: to regroup numbers when adding or multiplying

categories: groups based on similarities

census: an official count of an entire group, such as all the people in a nation

common denominators: denominators that are the same in two or more fractions

compare: to find out which number is larger or smaller

compatible pairs: sets of two numbers that divide equally

consumed: eaten or drunk up; used up

continuous: not ending

conversion factor: a number that a measurement is multiplied or divided by in order to convert from one unit to another

convert: to change from one unit to another without changing the value of the measurement

cross products: the results of multiplying the numerator of one fraction by the denominator of the other in a proportion

data: a collection of numbers that gives information about a subject

decimal point: the point that separates whole numbers from parts of a whole or dollars from cents

denominator: the bottom number in a fraction; tells how many parts the whole is divided into

diameter: the distance across a circle through the center of the circle

difference: the result when one number is subtracted from another

digit: a numeral between 0 and 9

dividend: the number being divided up in a division problem; the number inside the long division sign

estimate: to find a number that is close but not exact

factor: a number that is multiplied by another number to form a product; any number that another number is evenly divisible by; for example, factors of 4 are 1, 2, 4

formulas: equations or statements that show the constant relationship between values

front-end estimation: a method of estimating with large numbers by using only the first digits of the numbers

greatest common factor: the largest factor that two different numbers share; for example, the greatest common factor of 8 and 12 is 4.

improper fraction: a fraction with a numerator equal to or greater than its denominator

ingredients: parts of a recipe or plan that are added to a mixture

key: information that helps interpret a graph

labels: words used to describe or identify

lead digits: the first (left) digits of numbers

mean: the average found by dividing a total of numbers by the quantity of numbers in the set

micrometer: a very precise measurement tool that finds distances as small as a thousandth of an inch

mixed number: a number made up of a whole number and a fraction

motor skills: the ability to use hands, arms, and legs in a productive way

multiple: the product of one number and another number; for example, multiples of 2 include 2, 4, 6, 8, 10...

numerator: the top number in a fraction; tells how many parts of the whole there are

odometers: instruments that measure distance traveled

perimeter: the distance around a shape

place values: the sizes of digits based on their position in a number

population: an entire group to be studied statistically

prefix: a group of letters added to the beginning of a word to change its meaning

products: the results when two or more numbers are multiplied together

productivity: the amount of usable product; often measured in terms of hours of labor or cost of materials

proportion: an expression that says two fractions are equal

quotient: the result when one number is divided by another

radius: half the diameter of a circle; the distance from the center to the edge of a circle

range: the values from the lowest number in a group to the highest

reciprocal: a fraction with numerator and denominator reversed

reconciliation sheet: a form that a store uses to record the flow of money at a cash register

regroup: to move an amount to or from a place value to complete a basic operation

remainder: the amount left after dividing two numbers that do not divide evenly; for example, $5 \div 2$ is 2 with a remainder of 1

round number: a number ending in 0

sample: a representative portion of a population

sort: to put items or numbers in groups based on their similarities or differences

specifications: details or descriptions that tell how something is to be constructed or made

spreadsheets: tables of rows and columns that organize and present data

square units: labels that express size in two dimensions (length and width)

standards: levels of excellence against which something or someone is judged or compared

statistics: the collection, organization, and interpretation of data

substitute: to insert a value in place of a variable

sum: the result when two or more numbers are added together

tally: to count and record an amount

teller balancing record: the form a teller uses to account for his or her cash at the end of a business day

tolerance: the amount by which a measure is allowed to vary

trends: general directions, courses, or tendencies

variable: a letter of the alphabet (such as a, b, or x) that stands for an unknown number

working adjustment fund: the difference between a teller's beginning balance and cash at the end of the day

Index

Reference Handbook

Math Basics

ADDING, NO REGROUPING

$$\begin{array}{r} 41{,}536 \\ +\ 24{,}332 \\ \hline 65{,}868 \end{array}$$

Line up the digits. Add from right to left.

ADDING WITH REGROUPING

$$\begin{array}{r} {}^{1}\ \ ^{1}\ \ \ \\ 746 \\ +\ 1517 \\ \hline 2263 \end{array}$$

- Add the ones column: $6 + 7 = 13$.
  Bring down the 3 to the answer.
  Regroup the 1 ten.
- Add the tens column: $1 + 4 + 1 = 6$.
- Add the hundreds column. $7 + 5 = 12$
  Bring down the 2. Regroup the 1 thousand.
- Add the thousands column: $1 + 1 = 2$.

ADDING WITH ZEROS

Where there are zeros in the numbers being added, add and regroup as usual.

$$\begin{array}{r} {}^{1}\ \ \ \\ 8009 \\ +\ 1703 \\ \hline 9712 \end{array}$$

- Add the ones column. $9 + 3 = 12$
  Bring down the 2. Regroup the 1 ten.
- Add the tens column: $1 + 0 + 0 = 1$.
- Add the hundreds column: $0 + 7 = 7$.
- Add the thousands column: $8 + 1 = 9$.

SUBTRACTING, NO REGROUPING

$$\begin{array}{r} 457 \\ -\ 326 \\ \hline 131 \end{array}$$

Line up the digits. Subtract from right to left.

SUBTRACTING WITH REGROUPING

$$\begin{array}{r} {}^{7\ 10\ 15} \\ 8\cancel{1}\cancel{5} \\ -\ 346 \\ \hline 469 \end{array}$$

- Subtract the ones column. You can't subtract 6 from 5, so regroup 1 ten from the tens column: $15 - 6 = 9$.
- Subtract the tens column. Since you regrouped, there are 0 tens. Regroup 1 hundred, which is 10 tens. $10 - 4 = 6$
- Subtract the hundreds: $7 - 3 = 4$.

SUBTRACTING WITH ZEROS

When there are zeros in the number you are subtracting from, regroup by moving left one digit at a time until there is a digit you can regroup from.

$$\begin{array}{r} {}^{5\ 9\ 9\ 10} \\ \cancel{6}\cancel{0}\cancel{0}\cancel{0} \\ -\ \ 345 \\ \hline 5655 \end{array}$$

- You can't take 5 from 0, and there is no 1 in the tens place to regroup.
- Move left to the first digit greater than 0. Regroup 1 thousand.
- Now you have 10 hundreds. Regroup 1 hundred to leave 9 hundreds and 10 tens.
- Regroup 1 ten to leave 9 tens and 10 ones. Then subtract.

Multiplying and Dividing by 10, 100, or 1000

- To multiply by 10, move the decimal point <u>one</u> place to the <u>right</u>.
- To multiply by 100, move the decimal point <u>two</u> places to the <u>right</u>.
- To multiply by 1000, move the decimal point <u>three</u> places to the <u>right</u>.

Examples: $35.9 \times 10 = 35.9 = 359$

$4.258 \times 100 = 4.258 = 425.8$

$35 \times 1000 = 35{,}000$ ⟵— *Add zeros in order to move the decimal point three places.*

The decimal point in a whole number is understood to come after the number.

- To divide by 10, move the decimal point <u>one</u> place to the <u>left</u>.
- To divide by 100, move the decimal point <u>two</u> places to the <u>left</u>.
- To divide by 1000, move the decimal point <u>three</u> places to the <u>left</u>.

Examples: $14.5 \div 10 = 14.5 = 1.45$

$32 \div 100 = 32 = .32$

$48 \div 1000 = 048 = .048$

Add the zero in order to move the decimal point three places.

Multiplying and Dividing with Zeros

Use zeros as placeholders when multiplying or dividing large numbers.

Example:
$$\begin{array}{r} 783 \\ \times\ \ 40 \\ \hline 31{,}320 \end{array}$$
⟵——— *Since $0 \times 783 = 0$, use a zero as a placeholder in the ones place, and continue to multiply by the tens digit.*

Example:

These zeros are placeholders since 0 and 2 cannot be divided by 9.

$$\begin{array}{r} 10{,}003 \\ 9\overline{)90{,}027} \\ \underline{9}\ \ \ \ \ \ \\ 0\ 027 \\ \underline{27} \\ 0 \end{array}$$

Decimal Place Value

ten thousands	thousands	hundreds	tens	ones	.	tenths	hundredths	thousandths	ten thousandths
____	____	____	____	____		____	____	____	____

Examples:

.1   one tenth

.01   one hundredth

.001   one thousandth

.0001   one ten thousandth

Rounding to a Given Place Value

To round a number to a given place value, underline the digit just to the right of that place value.

- If the digit is less than 5, the digit in the given place value remains the same. Turn the underlined digit and all following digits to zeros. (Do not write them if they follow the decimal point.)
- If the underlined digit is 5 or above, add 1 to the digit in the given place value, and change the following digits to zeros.

Example: Round 1065 to the nearest hundred.

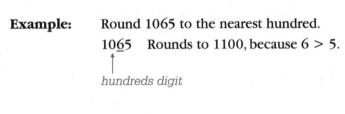

1065   Rounds to 1100, because 6 > 5.

hundreds digit

Example: Round 13.143 to the nearest tenth.

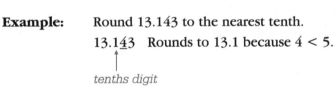

13.143   Rounds to 13.1 because 4 < 5.

tenths digit

Dividing by a Decimal

To divide by a decimal, you must first change the divisor (the number being divided by) to a whole number. To do this, move the decimal point as far to the right as you can. Then move the decimal point in the dividend (the number being divided up) the *same number of places.*

Example: $.05\overline{)2.405}$ becomes $5\overline{)240.5}$

Divide: $5\overline{)240.5}$ with quotient 48.1

Equivalent Fractions

You can find a fraction equivalent (equal) to another fraction by multiplying or dividing both numerator and denominator by the same number.

Example 1: $\frac{3}{4} \times \frac{3}{3} = \frac{9}{12}$

$$\frac{3}{4} \times \frac{3}{3} = \frac{3 \times 3}{4 \times 3} = \frac{9}{12}$$

$$\frac{3}{4} = \frac{9}{12}$$

Any number over itself is equal to 1. Multiplying by 1 does not change the value of a number.

Example 2: $\frac{18}{20} \div \frac{2}{2} = \frac{9}{10}$

$$\frac{18}{20} \div \frac{2}{2} = \frac{18 \div 2}{20 \div 2} = \frac{9}{10}$$

$$\frac{18}{20} = \frac{9}{10}$$

Any number over itself is equal to 1. Dividing by 1 does not change the value of a number.

To find an equivalent fraction with a given denominator, ask yourself, "What happened to the first denominator to get the second denominator?" Then apply the same operation to the numerator.

Example 3: $\frac{4}{7} = \frac{?}{21}$

Question: What happened to the 7 to get 21?
Answer: It was multiplied by 3.

$$\frac{4}{7} \times \frac{3}{3} = \frac{4 \times 3}{7 \times 3} = \frac{12}{21}$$

$$\frac{4}{7} = \frac{12}{21}$$

Finding the Lowest Common Denominator

For adding, subtracting, or even comparing, fractions need to have a common, or same, denominator. Using the lowest common denominator possible will make your work simpler.

Often, the lowest common denominator for two fractions is the larger of the two denominators.

Example: $\frac{2}{5} + \frac{7}{10}$ *Use 10 as the lowest common denominator.*

$$\frac{2}{5} = \frac{4}{10}$$
$$+\frac{7}{10} = \frac{7}{10}$$
$$\frac{11}{10} = 1\frac{1}{10}$$

If the larger of two denominators does not work as the lowest common denominator, try finding the *least common multiple* of the two denominators.

Example: $\frac{3}{4} + \frac{1}{10}$

What are the multiples of 4?   4, 8, 12, 16, 20, 24 ...

20 is the least common multiple.

What are the multiples of 10?   10, 20, 30, 40 ...

20 is the lowest common denominator.

$$\frac{3}{4} = \frac{15}{20}$$
$$+\frac{1}{10} = \frac{2}{20}$$
$$\frac{17}{20}$$

Canceling

When multiplying fractions, if a numerator and denominator have a common factor, you can make them easier to work with. To do this, simplify by canceling.

Example: $\frac{\overset{2}{\cancel{4}}}{5} \times \frac{3}{\underset{5}{\cancel{10}}} = \frac{6}{25}$ *The numerator 4 and the denominator 10 are both divisible by 2. Divide both numbers by 2, then multiply across as with any fraction multiplication problem.*

Reducing to Lowest Terms

You often need to simplify a fraction to lowest terms. Find the greatest common factor, and simplify both the numerator and denominator by the same amount.

Example: $\frac{4}{16}$ *Both 2 and 4 can be used as factors. Choose the largest: 4.*

$$\frac{4}{16} = \frac{4 \div 4}{16 \div 4} = \frac{1}{4}$$

You may also need to change an improper fraction to a mixed number.

Example: $\frac{23}{10}$ *Think:* $\frac{10}{10} = 1$.
10 divides into 23 two times with 3 left over.

$$\frac{23}{10} = \frac{20}{10} + \frac{3}{10} = 2\frac{3}{10}$$

Common Decimal, Fraction, and Percent Equivalents

Decimal	Fraction	Percent
.1	$\frac{1}{10}$	10%
.2	$\frac{1}{5}$	20%
.25	$\frac{1}{4}$	25%
.3	$\frac{3}{10}$	30%
.4	$\frac{2}{5}$	40%
.5	$\frac{1}{2}$	50%
.6	$\frac{3}{5}$	60%
.7	$\frac{7}{10}$	70%
.75	$\frac{3}{4}$	75%
.8	$\frac{4}{5}$	80%
.9	$\frac{9}{10}$	90%
1.0	$\frac{10}{10}$	100%

Changing Decimals, Fractions, and Percents

To change a decimal to a percent	To change a fraction to a percent	To change a percent to a decimal	To change a percent to a fraction
Move the decimal point two places to the right, and add a % sign. .70 = 70% 3.5 = 350% .009 = .9%	Divide the numerator by the denominator, then move the decimal point two places to the right, and add a percent sign. $\frac{1}{8} = ?\,\%$ $\begin{array}{r} .125 \\ 8\overline{)1.000} \\ \underline{8} \\ 20 \\ \underline{16} \\ 40 \\ \underline{40} \\ 0 \end{array}$ .125 = 12.5%	Move the decimal point two places to the left, and drop the percent sign. 35% = .35 .5% = .005 120% = 1.2	Drop the percent sign, and put the percent over 100. 53% = $\frac{53}{100}$ 75% = $\frac{75}{100}$ = $\frac{3}{4}$

Measurement Basics

Abbreviations					
in. = inch ft. = foot yd. = yard mi. = mile	oz. = ounce c. = cup pt. = pint qt. = quart gal. = gallon	oz. = ounce lb. = pound	mm = millimeter cm = centimeter m = meter km = kilometer	ml = milliliter l = liter	g = gram kg = kilogram

Equivalent Amounts					
12 in. = 1 ft. 3 ft. = 1 yd. 36 in. = 1 yd.	8 oz. = 1 c. 2 c. = 1 pt. 2 pt. = 1 qt. 4 c. = 1 qt. 4 qt. = 1 gal.	16 oz. = 1 lb.	10 mm = 1 cm 100 cm = 1 m 1000 m = 1 km	1000 ml = 1 l	1000 g = 1 kg

Multiplying and Dividing Measurements

Remember to convert measurements *after* multiplying.

9 inches $\times$ 6 = 54 inches   *Convert to feet by dividing by 12: 54 $\div$ 12 = 4 r 6.*

54 inches = 4 feet 6 inches, or $4\frac{1}{2}$ feet

Remember to convert measurements *before* dividing.

3 pounds $\div$ 8 ounces = ?   *Multiply 3 pounds by 16 to convert to ounces.*

3 $\times$ 16 = 48 ounces

48 $\div$ 8 = **6 ounces**

Common Formulas

Perimeter (P = perimeter)	**Square** $P = 4s$ (where s = side)	**Rectangle** $P = 2l + 2w$ (where l = length and w = width)	**Circle** $C = \pi d$ (where C = circumference, $\pi \approx 3.14$, d = diameter)
Area (A = area)	**Square** $A = s^2$ (where s = side)	**Rectangle** $A = lw$ (where l = length and w = width)	**Circle** $A = \pi r^2$ (where $\pi \approx 3.14$ and r = radius)
Volume (V = volume)	**Cube** $V = s^3$ (where s = side)	**Rectangular Solid** $V = lwh$ (where l = length, w = width, and h = height)	**Cylinder** $V = \pi r^2 h$ (where $\pi \approx 3.14$, r = radius, and h = height)

Solving Equations

The goal in solving any equation is to get the variable alone on one side of the equal sign. To do this, use inverse operations. Inverse operations undo other operations. For example, subtraction is the inverse of addition. Multiplication is the inverse of division.

Example: $x - 9 = 15$

The inverse of subtraction is addition. Therefore, *add* 9 to *both sides* of the equation.

$$x - 9 + 9 = 15 + 9$$

Then simplify: $x = 15 + 9 = 24$

Example: $x \times 3 = 18$

The inverse of multiplication is division. Therefore, *divide* by 3 on *both sides* of the equation.

$$x \times 3 \div 3 = 18 \div 3$$

Then simplify: $x = 18 \div 3 = 6$

Whatever you do to one side of an equation, you must do to the other side.

Calculator Basics

To use a calculator, press (key in) a number, an operation sign, then another number. Then press the equal sign. The answer will appear on the display. To erase what is on the display, press the Clear key (C). Always use the clear key between problems.

Commonly Used Keys

$-$	$+$	$\div$	$\times$	C	$=$	$\cdot$
subtract	add	divide	multiply	clear	equals	decimal point

Entering Basic Problems

	KEY IN	DISPLAY
$53 + 72$	C 5 3 + 7 2 =	125.
$89 - 37$	C 8 9 − 3 7 =	52.
$.5 \times .7$	C · 5 × · 7 =	0.35

Shows there are no whole numbers.

	KEY IN	DISPLAY
$60 \div 12$	C 6 0 ÷ 1 2 =	5.